THE
PHONY
HERMIT

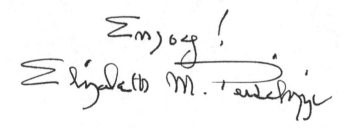

BY AL SEELY

EDITED & PUBLISHED:
ELIZABETH M. PERDICHIZZI

Al Seely Willie & Barbie, 1962 (Courtesy of Bob Steele)

Dock at Dismal Key (Courtesy of Bob Steele)

THE PHONY HERMIT

Graphics and Layout: Bill Perdichizzi

First Edition

© 2010

Library of Congress Card Number 2010939877
ISBN 978-0-9677281-7-9

Caxambas Publishing
1200 Butterfly Court
Marco Island, Florida 34145

Acknowledgements

The principal purpose of this book is the publication of the manuscript of Al Seely, who spent ten years living as a hermit on various keys in the Ten Thousand Islands. He knew that he was not a real hermit and entitled his work "The Phony Hermit."

In telling his story of survival in the wild you will discover as I did, that Al Seely is funny, charming, brutally honest, and totally human. His narrative, in the form of a black three-ring notebook containing 270 double-spaced, single-sided pages, came to light fifteen years after his death, and is now being published six years later.

The notebook was found in the backroom storage area of the Marco Island Chamber of Commerce when the staff was cleaning house. Chamber officials were at a loss of what they should do with it.

The notebook was given to me because of my interest in island lore and perhaps because I had authored and published two books on local history. I found the manuscript compelling and read it straight through. After checking with the Chamber, I began my search for family members to see if it had ever been published.

I wish to thank Charlotte Seely, Al's ex wife, for helping me locate his sister and brother-in-law, who put me in touch with Mark Cowell, Al Seely's son.

I am indebted to Mark for permission to publish his father's unvarnished work. Mark's long emails about his father serve as a wonderful introduction to the book and make a satisfying conclusion, that Al himself seemed to struggled with.

I am grateful to the Everglades High School students for permission to use the photographs from their booklet "Prop Roots, Vol. II Hermits from The Mangrove Country of The Everglades", published in 1980.

I wish to thank Joe and Ivy Douglas of Goodland, longtime friends from the Sailing Association of Marco Island for contributing knowledge of Al Seely after he came ashore to live in Goodland. They gave permission to publish the photos of Al Seely's original paintings on their window shades.

Thanks also to Bob Steele and his brother Dewey for sending personal photographs and anecdotes of their visits to Dismal Key.

PREFACE

"When my father first moved to the blue tent on Brush Key, I don't think anyone, including himself, thought he'd last very long.

"At that time, he was a late stage, chronic alcoholic - and I say that with great love and affection because I have shared the same disease and the same genes as my old man. But my own legacy of alcoholism was just getting off the ground at college parties at Northeastern University when his was grinding toward a potentially tragic finish. He had been diagnosed with cirrhosis of the liver and given only a short time to live. He was unemployable, on welfare, and dying of alcoholism.

"His decision to leave society and become a hermit was not done out of a sense of adventure but out of a combination of despair and grabbing for straws. I'm not sure that he didn't intend to just go out there and die. I expected that he'd stay for a week, give it up, and try something else.

"He stayed for ten years."

Mark Cowell
Al Seely's son

Al Seely on Dismal Key, June 1972 (Courtesy of Bob Steele)

TABLE OF CONTENTS

Chapter 1

Getting it together

a: Where?

Dock And Path Leading Up To Al Seely's House On Dismal Key
(Photo courtesy of Everglades City High School students)

As unlikely as it may sound, the tropical island where my dog "Digger" and I live now is called "Dismal Key." No kidding!

You can find it on any nautical chart for the coastline south of Naples, Florida. (For example, Department of Commerce Nautical Chart 642-SC.) Not having a chart, you can look at a road map of Florida or even an adequate atlas and, directing your attention to the southwest coast, you will find this area designated as the Ten Thousand Islands. Dismal Key is located in the midst of this strange but beautiful wilderness about halfway between Goodland and Everglades City.

People often ask how Dismal Key got its lugubrious name. I wish I knew. But, since I haven't as yet turned up even a clue, I suggest that they visit me during July or August when the heat, the mosquitoes, and the sand flies are at their rip-roaring best and they will at least discover why it's not called Paradise Key.

So, Dismal Key is one of the Ten Thousand Islands. But it's more than just another mangrove island. It has at its northwest tip a pile of seashells, mostly oyster shells. If you want to boggle your mind a bit, imagine a pile of oyster shells about sixteen feet high covering an area of sixty-five acres. That's the kind of pile I'm talking about. What's more, they are not here by accident or through some freak of nature. They were piled up over the years … maybe even over the centuries … by patient, hard working hands: Calusa Indian hands, to be specific. Right on. It's an Indian shell mound. Of course it is now covered with a luxurious jungle growth with many huge trees, shrubs, plants and vines beyond counting, and so it does not in any way look like a pile of shells, though basically that's what it is.

Coming up Dismal Channel to this mound you will first see a skinny-looking dock sticking out into the water, then a little green boathouse near which several mostly decrepit boats are lying about. One little aluminum boat should be bobbing in the water beside the dock, tied to a buttonwood stump. If it's not there …I ain't to home. That's my boat … the others belong to friends.

Then, there is a little dirt footpath leading up the sixteen-foot hill, which is no mean hill in these parts, by the way. It winds between clumps of cactus liberally spattered with yellow flowers or red or green fruit, past another oddly squat building with a rusty, tin roof, which is my cistern. Then comes a huge, crazy-branched Royal Poinciana tree, which is a mass of orange-red blooms in early summer, past some red-barked Gumbo Limbo trees and a salmon-flowered hibiscus. The path then reaches the rickety front stoop of an ancient wooden house that in all it's fifty or sixty years has never known a coat of paint, yet has a certain weathered beauty.

Al Seely's house on Dismal Key
(Photo courtesy of Everglades City High School students)

The previous occupant of this house, a hermit I will introduce to you later on, used to say: "Hermits have it better than anybody; look at me with a two bedroom, split level, waterfront home."

I can't use that description anymore because when I moved in, I had to remodel one of the so-called bedrooms to make an indoor toilet. It's not that I am squeamish about using the original smelly outhouse, but I couldn't stand upright in it (he was only five-four to my six feet in height). Nor can I get my fat ass to fit the hole, which is too close to the wall. He had only the barest hip bones to hang his pants on whereas I lug around over 200 pounds, most of which is below the neck and above the knees. I am undoubtedly the only flab-fat hermit in existence.

~

Al Seely In Front Of His House
(Photo courtesy of Everglades City High School students)

Just as I'll tell you more about the other little hermit, I'll also later go into some detail about this house, but for now...

Main Room On Dismal Key
(Photo courtesy of Everglades City High School students)

Bedroom On Dismal Key
(Photo courtesy of Everglades City High School students)

This is my home.
This is where.

b: Who?

Al Seely
(Photo courtesy of Everglades City High School students)

Well, my name is Al Seely. Al for Albert, which I detest. If my name had been Mike or Peter or Doug, I would probably be a corporation president today instead of a hermit. But Albert, yuck!

I am also known as the Hermit of Dismal Key.

I sometimes receive mail addressed to Artist, Dismal Key, or Artist, Ten Thousand Islands.

A couple of smart-asses call me *The Man* of Dismal Key.

My name is correct. But, I don't know about the hermit part. The American Heritage Dictionary says a hermit is a person who has withdrawn from society and lives a solitary existence. This poses a nit-pick. I live a solitary existence, by that I mean that no one shares the island with me but my dog; and my place of residence is miles from society, but society comes to me. Friends, tourists, amateur archaeologists, photographers, fishermen, Sunday boaters, rich and poor, celebrities and nonentities, they come by two's and four's and more ... forty or fifty a month. I enjoy every sociable minute of it, which I shouldn't if I'm a true recluse. If I'm a hermit, I'm certainly a phony one. Perhaps as we go along I can show how this strange development took place.

I am not an artist either, in the conventional sense of the word. Self taught, I do paint and sell many pictures of a schlock-art type, but nothing truly creative.

No mayor, certainly. If there's to be a mayor here, it would have to be Digger. He has all the qualifications: he tries to kiss everybody, he holds center stage at all times, and he makes a lot of noise without saying anything. Digger for Mayor!

If, then, I am not a hermit, an artist, or mayor, what am I?

I suspect I am really a bit of a basket case, else why the hell would I be out here on an Indian Mound with my bugs, rats, rattlesnakes, scorpions, birds, animals, and one goddam crocodile, when I could be enjoying the comforts and conveniences of urban living? Why, I could be in a three bedroom, two bath, thrice mortgaged, highly taxed home. Or, I could be driving an unpaid-for car, breathing smog and fumes in bumper-to-bumper traffic. Or I could be listening to the soothing sounds of police sirens, diesel truck engines, and teenagers burning rubber with their motorcycles. Or, I could be sitting before the tube being edified by crime and comedy, deodorized, with a fresh application of Preparation H up my ass, and munching Rolaids.

c: Why?

The question I am most often asked by my visitors is, "Why did you decide to leave everything and come out here to live a more or less primitive life?" This question takes many forms, of course, but that is the essence of it. I am always intrigued by the various circumlocutions and tangential approaches to it. Often it begins," I know this isn't any of my business, but ...," or "I wonder if you'd mind awfully giving me just a rough idea of why...," etc. What do you suppose they expect to hear? That I am a fugitive wanted for raping old ladies in six states? Or that I have a whiskey still and raise pot back in the woods? Or that I practice Zen Buddhism or black magic? Do they really expect me to admit I'm a zany?

At first I used to tell half-truths. I would say that I got fed up with civilization and the rat race and came out for some peace and quiet, which is true, as far as it goes. I'd say that my wife has five cats and seven dogs, and that though I love dogs, seven is too d... many and I hate cats. This is also true, but not the essential truth. Lately, though, I have given up all this wool pulling and just come right out with it – bang! I am here because I am an alcoholic trying to manage my booze intake. I explain that being miles from the nearest town with only a tiny boat for transportation, not always having money in my pocket, I get along much better than when I could pop around the corner to the nearest convenience store for a jug of wine and when I could always hock something for the necessary bucks.

d. When and How?

Having disposed of who I am, where I am, and why I am here, we come to the when. When and how did I begin to decide to abandon civilization and trek into the wilderness?

Well, I don't know when. You see, I was drunk at the time. I had been in my usual drunken stupor for several days and was just reaching that point in all my bouts when my system rebels and signals the foggy remnants of my brain that it's time to quit. This is a very frightening time because I begin to realize that I am about to go through several days of withdrawal hell. So on this occasion, whenever it was, and in that semi-awakening state, I found myself chanting as if it were a mantra, "I gotta get a fuckin' boat. I gotta get a fuckin' boat," and so on, pounding the table with my fist for emphasis and also to establish the beat. Usually, I don't remember much of what I do or say or think when I'm drunk. But this time, after I had pulled through the tunnel of horrors, I recalled that "fuckin' boat" routine. I told Charlotte about it.

Charlotte is my ex-wife who in those days was kind enough to take me in after my drunks and feed me Librium and hot soup and assure me that the crabs on the ceiling wouldn't bite me.

"What do you suppose I want a boat for?" I asked her.

"Boy, that is all you need ... to have a boat to get drunk in," she sniffed.

"But that's just the point, " I argued. "A boat is supposed to help me in some way, but damned if I know how, unless I lived in one out in the middle of the ocean somewhere."

"I don't know," she said. "You've had a trailer on a woodlot to get drunk in and a station wagon with an air mattress for the same purpose. Now you have a trailer in a trailer park. You've used up your welcome in all the surrounding motels and hotels. I was even trying to help you buy a house, as you recall. So now you want a boat?"

"Yeah," I mumbled. "I guess it's pretty ridiculous at that."

So, that exchange didn't get us anywhere.

I tried to let it go as just another inebriated insanity, but somehow it stuck in my mind and I found myself twisting and stretching it for some meaning.

"Boat" eventually evolved into "houseboat," but I wondered what good, if any, would it do me to live on a houseboat? And anyway, from a practical standpoint, I realized that boats or houseboats cost money: hundreds, maybe thousands of dollars, which ruled them out right there even if they should guarantee complete sobriety, which they didn't.

It then began to edge into my consciousness that what I needed was not a boat *per se*, but a means of getting away from it all. This led to dreams of a log cabin in the forest of northern Maine or out in the mountains of Montana. I began studying the atlas, searching for areas of low population density. In some of my far-out moments, even Afghanistan or Siberia looked promising. Apparently, I needed to get away from people as well as from an easy booze supply. I guess I had such a low opinion of myself at the time that it had to follow that everyone else was a shit-ass too!

But Maine, Montana, or Afghanistan, all were equally out of the question without having a whole bunch of money. So, get closer to home: the tropics, easy living. How about the Everglades; the Big Cypress Swamp? Closer to possibility, but even there I'd need a shack, a swamp buggy or a jeep, or some damn way to get out for supplies. But I knew that even if I could get located out in the swamp, I'd probably manage to get drunk sometime or other, and I could see myself lurching through the saw grass, slopped to the chops, stepping on rattlesnakes, or tripping over an alligator. So, no Everglades. No way.

By this time, however, the idea that I had to get away somewhere had become an obsession with me. I began to cast up tentative budgets, watch the ads for used jeeps and even boats. That damned boat idea was still lodged in my cranium.

Then one evening, after studying the map of Florida for the umpteenth time, my eyes kept coming back to the southwest coast and the Ten Thousand Islands. If I could live on one of those islands...

Charlotte came out of the bathroom just then with a towel around her freshly washed hair. I called her over to show her the map.

"Hey, I think I've got it," I said.

"Got what?"

"A place to live. Out in the wilderness by myself. See here, this area called the Ten Thousand Islands? Here's a road leading into the town of Goodland. Way down here is one leading into Everglades City. But, in between, there is no way to get in or out except by boat."

"I can see that all right," she agreed, "but what would you live in once you got there?"

Good question. I scratched my nose until a thought came along.

"Why not a tent?" I suggested. "Maybe I could buy a secondhand tent somewhere. And I wouldn't need much of a boat. Some little ole pram or something."

"Well, maybe..." she thought a minute. "But, what could you do ... I mean, how could you live? You have to eat, you know."

It was my turn to think a minute.

Then I heard myself saying, "Why, I'd live off the land." Then I cried, "Hey, that's not bad. You know, during the depression back in the Thirties, my family lived (well, practically lived) on dandelions and milkweed greens and blueberries and stuff like that. We even made our own maple sugar. Of course, that was up in New England, but maybe even in Florida you could find ..."

"I could afford to help you some, I guess, " Charlotte went on, ignoring my brainstorm. By this time I had yakked about my schemes to go off somewhere so continually that she had come to believe that it might actually be the best thing for me. Being a woman, her approach to the business was much more practical.

"Well, why couldn't I live off the land?" I insisted.

"What? Oh, I don't know; maybe you could."

"No harm in finding out," I concluded.

I began with letters to several Florida universities and Government agencies like the Marine Biology Laboratory at Woods Hole, Massachusetts. I scoured the library and bookstores. One weekend we took a trip down to Flamingo, the tourist center of the Everglades National Park. Here, I had my first glimpse of wild terrain similar to what I might expect to find where I was going. We hiked the nature trails and took a boat trip through mangrove island country, I picked up a pot full of miscellaneous information but not much on edible plants except for one great book which I found on sale at the park Headquarters: *Wild Plants for Survival in South Florida* by Julia F. Morton. This became my Bible, still is whenever I want to look up some possible edible.

When I discovered that Mrs. Morton was connected with the University of Miami as Director of the "Morton Collectanea;" I pumped up enough courage to write her about my hopes to rough it in the islands. She was kind enough to grant me an interview, which added greatly to my slowly growing fund of information.

Possibly, the most important thing I learned from her was never to eat any plant, fruit, or anything that I was not sure of. It seems that some plant toxins are pretty sneaky. They don't always make you sick right away maybe not for a day or two, by which time you can be close to terminal. I shudder to think what might have happened to me if I'd gone about sampling everything indiscriminately as I intended to do.

I wrote to the Chamber of Commerce at Everglades City to inquire about possible campsites and camping restrictions, or permits required in the islands. When I got a reply informing me that there were quite a few camping beaches and that no permits were required outside of the National Park, I really got to work making lists, and starting to shop.

The trick here was not to compile such a complete list of stuff that I would never have to worry about any contingency, but to cut the damn list down so that I would be able to get everything with three hundred dollars. Don't laugh that was my budget! Absolute tops, counting both what few bucks I could earn driving cab on the nights I was sober, and what Charlotte felt she could contribute.

And I did it too.

It took months. First, I kept drinking up my cab money and would have to go out and earn it all over again. As a matter of fact, I got so discouraged over this stupidity that I might never have reached my goal at all if Charlotte hadn't somehow kept my hopes up. Then it took time to find things like a good used tent large enough to live in and a decent secondhand shotgun.

Eventually, believe it or not, I got my "fuckin' boat." It was no houseboat, cabin cruiser, or any other dream type boat; it was only a ten-foot aluminum Jon boat with a three and one half horse motor. But it was a boat. My other gear consisted of an axe, machete, footlocker, folding camp cot, beat up card table, folding chair, water jugs, skillet, pots, can openers, and candles. Fortunately, I didn't need many clothes. The basic Florida wardrobe is T-shirt, blue jeans, and tennis shoes. I did indulge in a pair of leather boots and some snake-proof puttees.

Finally, all that was left was to take a deep breath and shove off.

Chapter 2

Getting Launched

There was a gray cotton fog early in the morning on New Year's Day of 1967 as Charlotte drove us into Chokoloskee, her old yellow Dodge dragging ass under the inverted Jon boat tied to the roof, the trunk and back seat packed like two cans of tuna with the rest of my gear.

Chokoloskee?

Yeah. Well … We went to Everglades City first since that was where the friendly Chamber of Commerce was located, also the Park Ranger's office. Since I didn't know how to go about finding one of those suitable camping islands, I figured the Park Ranger could help. Apparently, he was helping somebody else, since we couldn't find him. As I stood beside our Okie rig scratching my head, a native ambled along eyeballing us. He grinned and said, "Howdy."

"Howdy," I said.

Then he stopped and said, "'Scuse me, but you all look like you might be havin' a 'predicalment.'"

"On the button," I agreed. "I'm looking for the Park Ranger."

"W'all," he drawled, "youall might mosey on daown to Chokoloskee. Likely smell him out there."

That's how come Chokoloskee.

And we didn't find him there either.

A friendly motel owner listened to the problem and allowed as how it wasn't a big one. I could just go out to Comer Key and set up my tent and all. He was sure the Ranger wouldn't mind a helluva lot. Then I could scout around for a permanent campsite.

"Thanks very much," I said. "But would you mind telling me how to get to Comer Key and approximately how far it is?"

"Well, tain't much more'n five-six-mile, I reckon. You cut across the bay there and hit that narr river." He proceeded to give me at least four alternative routes, which meant absolutely nothing except the across-the-bay-part. Hell, I could see across the bay. But just as I started to panic he said, "Ok, iffn you want, you kin just foller the markers."

Ahhh.

He also allowed us to park, unload, and get launched at his dock at no charge. I never did get to camp on Comer Key, though, and it wasn't because of the fog.

By the time I had gotten my little ten-foot Jon boat launched with three and one-half horsepower motor attached and gassed up, and a heavy footlocker full of clothes aboard, the fog had lifted enough so that even a landlubber like me could pick out the channel markers that I had to follow.

Charlotte gave me a kiss and wished me luck as I shoved off. She told me later that as she watched me chugging my way out into the maze of islands, she never expected to see me again. But I made the five or so miles out to Comer Key and the trip back with a minimum of difficulty. There were a few boners, of course, like when in a wide area of the bay I could not only see the marker immediately in front of me, but the one beyond that which was off to the right. It never occurred to me that there was a good reason for them to be positioned like that. I simply figured it would be a clever idea to head for the second one and save some time, the shortest distance between two points and all that. I learned my first lesson right there: never try to save time by cheating channel markers! I ran smack onto a mud flat and not only had to row fifty yards to deeper water, but lost ten minutes pulling the starter rope on my motor which had stalled.

I ran into mud a second time further out when I got so engrossed in watching a couple of half grown raccoons feeding along the edge of a small mangrove island that I forgot to watch where I was going. But another goof was more serious. When I arrived at Comer Key I had only one thought in mind, to take my footlocker ashore, hide it safely, and get on back for my next load. I got it on my back like the pirates of old, stumped up the beach, and stashed it in a thick clump of bushes. If I had looked around me at all I'd have likely seen the huge sign which said "NO CAMPING, order of the Park Department" or words to that effect. And if I had noticed that sign I would not have left the footlocker which was never seen again, nor would I have tried to make a second trip, the trip which changed the whole picture. But I didn't see it.

Immediately after an early lunch I was again sputtering down the channel with the second load, keeping all the markers in strict one – two - three order. I was almost lightheaded from drinking in the beauty of this strange country and from the increasing surge and boil of my enthusiasm. But there was one change. A breeze had sprung up with it a light chop on the water. A Jon boat has a square prow, as you probably know, and before long the little waves were splashing against it and spattering the cardboard box of canned goods I had on the bow seat.

"Well," I figured, "if I shut her down I'll likely have to spend another ten minutes on the starter rope, so let's see if it will steer itself a bit."

Whereupon, I let go of the steering handle and stooped forward to move the box. My two hundred pounds-plus and the next wave hit the front of the boat at the same instant. The next thing I knew, like a submarine in a power dive, we were heading straight for the bottom!

I will never forget the sensation I experienced at that moment. There was no fear in it for some curious reason. It was simply the damnedest feeling of utter helplessness. As I stared stupidly down at the water rushing up my legs and hips my mind seemed to be yelling, "No! It ain't true. No! No!"

For all I knew I could have been heading for Davy Jones' locker in forty fathoms, so when the boat came gently to rest on the bottom in three and one-half feet of water, I must have been relieved. But all I can remember is that I stood there with my mouth hanging open watching my gear float away. Finally, it began to come through to me that no matter how much I disbelieved it; the true gist of the situation was that I was standing out there in the middle of Chokoloskee Channel up to my middle in water.

I looked around then to get my bearings and found that I was actually not more than a hundred yards from shore and that on the shore was a house and a dock, and on the dock a man was fishing. I flapped my arms around and yelled. All that I could think of to yell right off was, "Hey." So I yelled, "Hey!" When there was no noticeable response from the guy, I yelled, "Hey!" again, louder. Still nothing.

"I suddenly found myself sinking with water up to my chest"

Now that situation is not designed for prolonged contemplation ... for a guy to stand with his finger up his ass so to speak. It demanded action ... any kind of action. So I acted; I stepped out of the boat and sank another two feet into the muck, where I stuck fast. The reason I did that was that I remembered my boat had a built in flotation and I thought if I got out of it, it might come to the surface. It came up all right, upside down, but I managed to grab it before it floated away too. I yelled, "Hey!" a couple of more times and on a much higher and hysterical note. Stuck in the mud I couldn't even swim anywhere, and I was beginning not to like it very much. Unfortunately, I never had a chance to apologize to that fisherman for all the uncomplimentary four letter things I called him when he just stood there fishing, and watching me like it was everyday that he saw some poor schnook floundering around out in the bay with an overturned boat. But the reason he didn't do anything was because he had told someone else in the house about my plight. At least I guess that's what he must have done, because in not over five minutes, three boats were heading to my rescue. A couple of big bruisers in the first boat pulled me out of the mud and flopped me aboard like a hooked dolphin while the others cruised around collecting my oars and the three boxes and cans that were still afloat.

In no time, the "would-be-hermit" was right back on the motel dock where he started. Charlotte, who had watched the whole drama from the channel bank, greeted me with a mixture of relief and concern.

"Are you all right?" she wanted to know.

"Yeah. I'm fine," I told her as I stood dripping in the middle of a pile of soggy cartons and a ruined motor. "Just fine."

~

On the first Saturday in February 1967, the undaunted, would-be hermit arrived in Goodland, Florida ready to strike out again. In case you're wondering why I didn't go back to Chokoloskee for my second attempt, I can only confess that after my ignominious upset in the bay, after going back the following week to recover my footlocker and finding it gone, and at the same time discovering that big "No Camping" sign on Comer Key, I felt like such a complete d… fool that I couldn't face the Chokoloskee citizenry again. Not only that, but during the month of refurbishing, I had decided to charter a boat big enough to carry me and the whole caboodle, to wherever I was going, in one trip. I had also decided to keep out of the National Park altogether, which meant that Goodland would be a closer jumping off point.

Goodland as it looked in 1959

22

In fact, the day I went back to retrieve the footlocker I went on up to Goodland to reconnoiter. There, I met a most obliging charter boat captain who sat down with me over a copy of the local chart and helped me select a suitable island. He also agreed to ferry me out to it whenever I was ready. This second attempt then was much better planned and so - it succeeded.

It might make my adventures a bit more colorful if, at this point, I take time out to describe this unique corner of our world.

To begin with, anyone not familiar with south Florida might conclude that going off to live on a deserted island anywhere off the coast here would be on a par with taking a Sunday jaunt into the country for a picnic. Such a conclusion would be quite inaccurate. The southern tip of Florida is almost completely a vast wilderness area. True, there is the famous gold coast of Miami, Miami Beach, Ft. Lauderdale, the Palm Beaches and so on, but this entire conglomerate of overpopulation covers only a thin strip of land along the lower east coast. On the west coast, the southernmost city of any size is Naples. Below that, Marco Island, Goodland, Everglades City, and Chokoloskee are but tiny communities clinging to the edge of the Everglades. Between the east and west coast areas of population there lies a vast and formidable expanse of swamps, saw grass, endless streams and hammocks, except that on the southwest coastline the swamps give way to a great line of mangrove islands stretching well over a hundred miles from Naples to Flamingo. The upper part of this chain is known as the Ten Thousand Islands, and if I'm any judge from having lived here, I'd say that was a short count.

This complex of islands and swamp is the only area of its kind in the world. Some have called it the last true wilderness in the United States; others refer to it as America's last frontier. From the ecological standpoint it is tremendously important since it supports such a variety of wildlife from mosquitoes and gnats all the way up to and including bears, panthers, and deer. It also abounds in snakes, turtles, alligators, and hundreds of bird species. And the intermingling of fresh and salt-water areas along the west coast provide the unique conditions that are vital to the proliferation of fish and other aquatic life.

For the most part, the thousands of mangrove islands are no more and no less than aggregations of red mangrove trees (*Rhizophora mangle* L.). They range in size anywhere from a clump of four or five small trees to some covering hundreds of acres with trees up to 60 feet in height.

The special feature of the red mangrove tree is its root structure. Each tree has many prop roots which grow out of the trunk above ground or water level and curve down to imbed themselves in whatever soil or muck is available. These roots usually subdivide, sometimes more than once. The result makes the tree look as if it were clutching the earth with a great handful of intertwining reddish fingers. When the trees grow close together as they do on these islands, the roots wind over, under, and around each other making a virtually impenetrable mass. And, as if the trees felt that all these bottom roots were still insufficient to hold them secure against hurricanes and high seas, they often sent out aerial roots, some from as high as 20 feet or more, which grown downward, branching and rebranching to join the mass at the base.

Another unique feature of these trees and roots is that around the perimeter of each island where the roots are exposed to the rise and fall of the tides, they are covered with great clusters of small oysters. For those who enjoy this culinary delight, as I do, there are literally millions of oysters to be had for the picking. They are small, but every bit as sweet and delicious as any you can procure elsewhere.

There are some exceptions to the general mangrove structure of these islands. Those which front the open Gulf of Mexico we call the "outside" islands, and due to the action of winds, tides, and currents, some of these have built up some high ground... high in this case being a matter of three to six feet above sea level. The accumulated sand, seashells and debris have formed a soil capable of supporting the growth of a large variety of trees, shrubs, and plants other than mangrove. A few of the "inside" island have high ground too, but that is invariably man made, constructed centuries ago by the prehistoric Calusa Indians out of tremendous piles of discarded seashells. Through centuries of decomposition these islands have also come to have fertile soil and a rich plant and animal life.

Around all these islands are miles and miles of waterways from tiny creeks too narrow for a canoe to pass through, to large bays and lakes. A special feature of all this water is that the average depth is no more than four feet, mostly less. Of course, there are many deeper channels where inland rivers flow out to the sea and deep holes here and there are scoured by stronger currents.

Wilderness or no, the island was not completely devoid of human habitation. I found after I got there that two other hermits were there: one living in the National Park on Possum Key, and one nearer to me, my predecessor on Dismal Key. The Possum Key hermit was in his nineties, the Dismal Key hermit in his seventies, leaving me, at 50, the baby in the lot. Two previous old loners who lived out here have gone, I hope, to hermit heaven.

Curiously enough, however, in exploring some of the Calusa shell mounds, I have found ancient cisterns attesting to the existence of white settlers in this area, probably a hundred years ago. One such mound located on the Pumpkin River has a cleared space of some few acres where definite traces of old plowed furrows may still be seen, and on Fahkahatchee Island, close to Everglades City, are the remains of a schoolhouse, several buildings, and even an old cemetery, all that remains of a community that existed there at some remote time.

People seeing all this for the first time often exclaim how beautiful it is. Being a pseudo-artist, I never dispute anyone's concept of beauty, but for my taste there is entirely too much monotony to the landscape. The trees grow to a uniform height, making for an unvarying skyline so that if you are in the center of one of the bays or lakes and look around, it is practically impossible to find any landmark to show where the entrance or exit may be. As a result, it is frightfully easy to get lost, especially since any given area looks considerably different at high tide than it does at low, or at different times of the day when shadows change. There are some, like the local mullet fishermen, who have an uncanny ability to find their way through this maze of islands in fog or in the dead of a moonless night, but I am not one of them. After many trials and more errors I have learned how to get where I have to go during daylight, and that's all.

This, then, is the country I was heading for on that first Saturday afternoon in February as we cruised out of Goodland toward the open water of Gullivan Bay, the boat heaped with all my camping gear and my little John boat bobbing happily along in the wake. We were making for Brush Key, a little island only a few miles from Goodland, which I was already beginning to think of as my island. I eventually settled much further from civilization, but my Chokoloskee fiasco had taken some of the edge off my derring-do, and I was quite content to get the hang of being a hermit a bit closer to stores and people.

As we approached the island I could see right off that it was going to be ideal, with its strip of beach and Gumbo Limbo trees indicating high ground. There was also a long oyster reef jutting out from the southern tip that I figured would make for good fishing. As we started to go right on past this reef I asked the captain:

"Isn't that where we're going … Brush Key?"

"That's right," he said, "but I can't put you ashore anywhere on this side. Water's too shallow. We'll swing around this here reef and cut back in on the other side. You'll see."

Sure enough, there was a short beach on the other side with water deep enough close in so that he was able to run the bow right onto the sand. He helped me unload my gear, then came ashore to look around. Casting a professional looking eye about, he said,

"Your lucky. Look at this nice, sandy beach to pitch your tent on."

"You think it'll be all right?" I asked. "It looks awful damn close to the water."

"Oh, sure," he insisted, pointing to a row of twigs, leaves, shells, and bits of seaweed, "See this line of stuff? That's your high tide line, you got plenty of room."

"I hope you're right," I said as I paid him, … "and thanks."

"Lots of luck to you," he told me as he climbed into his boat, "and if you ever need anything out here, just let me know."

"Okay, thanks again, I will. What's your phone number?"

That broke him up. "How about that!" he roared. "No phone lines out this way yet. Hah! Well, don't worry about a thing. I'll cruise by from time to time to see how you're making out."

As he backed off from shore, Willie and I started out on the reef to watch him out of sight.

Oh, Willie.

Willie was my first dog, a black retriever puppy, Willie, short for William Lumplumb. After a hearty wave as the boat rounded the reef and headed toward town, I squatted down to pat my puppy on the head.

"Well, Willie, old boy, here we are at last. Just the two of us on our own island."

A shiver went through me then as the reality of the situation dug into my consciousness. I was aware of being happy, excited, and afraid all at the same time. I can't express how deeply grateful I was at that moment for a little puppy dawg. He wagged his tail and rolled his soft, trusting brown eyes up at me, and truly, a love affair was born.

Among the dozens of thoughts crowding through my mind, the business about the lack of a telephone was uppermost. It had never occurred to me to wonder while planning this venture how I could get help if I should have a heart attack, break an arm or leg, or cut myself seriously with axe or machete. I hadn't even bothered to have a physical checkup to see if I was still in good condition, or to discover any incipient diseases that would make it risky to live alone on an island.

"Kinda' late for all that," I mumbled to myself, "we're here now."

But almost immediately my normal optimism asserted itself and I thought that it was a pretty fine thing to be free from telephones after all. There'd be no one bugging me about anything at all.

"Come on, pup, " I said. "We're going to be in top shape and I've got work to do."

~

Back on the beach, that little area of sand didn't quite measure up to what I felt a tent site should be, despite the Captain's recommendations. The only other spot nearby that was halfway adequate was covered with brush, but a glance at the sun assured me there was time enough to clear it before dark. Rummaging through my gear I found my machete and went to work. It didn't take too long to clear it and shovel enough sand over the spot to cover the sharp little stubs to keep them from poking through the tent floor, but it was long enough to work up an appetite. I cut a couple of small, green logs, dug a hole on the beach and lined them up, one of each side of it. I found the iron straps I brought along for the purpose and placed them crosswise on the logs to hold the cast iron skillet. A little fire and in no time, hot beans and corned beef were ready.

By the time the meal was over and the puppy fed, the sun had dropped several degrees closer to the horizon. Fortunately, my tent had an outside aluminum tubular frame, which doesn't take too much time to erect, but even so, by the time the stakes had been driven and the canvas spread and ready to go, it was getting dark. So much so, in fact, that I didn't notice that the tent was going up ass-end to: by which I mean that the tent door instead of facing the beach as anyone would have intended, was now facing the jungle. "To hell with it," I thought as I stumbled around my pile of gear, pulling out the army style folding cot and air mattress and poking into boxes in search of my candles, "I can change it tomorrow."

Eventually, things were squared away by candlelight, the mattress inflated, camp stool unfolded, a few boxes stored, and blankets unpacked. All the while Willie had been staring out through the screen door alternately barking and growling, his hackles stiff. I had been too busy to pay attention to him, but once there was nothing left to do but sit and look out at the jungle myself, I felt my own rudimentary hackles itching.

It was kind of spooky! A three-quarter moon shed just enough light to throw the great masses of jungle vines and brush into eerie highlights and inky shadows. Hurricane Donna, in 1961,[1] had come rampaging through the Ten Thousand Islands tossing trees around like toothpicks. These same trees, now dead and weathered to a shiny white, looked like giant's bones protruding at weird angles from the fetid growth below.

Now, I'm not unreasonably timid or fanciful, but at that moment all I could think of was the lecture I had attended at the Everglades National Park headquarters in which the Park Ranger had said that there were panthers, bears, wildcats, rattlesnakes and things like that in the Everglades. "But it's unlikely you will ever see any of them," he said. "Because they only venture out to hunt and prowl at night."

Night, eh? Suddenly my tent seemed like a very fragile barrier against these possible marauders. Willie must have thought so too the way he kept growling at real or imagined noises out there in the jungle, not four feet away. Once we both nearly jumped clean out of our skins at a wild scream that sounded like someone with acute laryngitis being strangled. I learned later to identify that raucous cry with the great white heron, but at the time it seemed more likely to have issued from some fiend out of hell.

But it was not a wild creature that ruined that night. You can imagine that alone and at night in that strange, wild environment, it wasn't easy to make myself believe that, after all, the jungle was just a big bluff … probably. Before long, however, fatigue began to sneak up on me. My eyes and mind both got droopy. I made sure my shotgun was loaded and ready to hand, before I blew out the candle and stretched out to sleep.

The next thing I knew, I was hearing a roaring sound and the tent walls were popping all over the place. A stiff wind had sprung up and with it, a heavy surf. As I struggled into my clothes I could hear the breakers crashing so close by I expected each one to sweep us tent and all, into the jungle. I found my spotlight, unzipped the door and edged fearfully around the tent to assess this new threat. It was a relief to find that the breakers were nowhere near as large as they sounded, but I noticed that the little strip of beach that was "just the place for my tent" was long gone. Even the fire hole and logs were gone.

---

[1] Editor Note: Hurricane Donna hit in 1960, not 1961.

But was this high tide, or hadn't it reached the flood yet? There was no way of knowing, or even guessing. I estimated the distance from the breakers to my tent as being about ten feet and the elevation as two, so I figured there'd be some time before the waves forced me to evacuate. Because that's all I could do, if it came to it; take what I could, crawl back into the jungle, and watch the rest of my stuff float away a second time; which reminded me of my boat. I went to check on it. I had tied it to a tree in a little cover nearby. Fortunately, it was rocking gently and safely, being sheltered from the frothing surf.

Back in the tent I got the candlelight. No sense in trying to sleep in that bedlam of wind and waves, which would bear watching anyway. Every half-hour or so I checked but apparently the tide was as high as it intended to go that night.

The wind, on the other hand, was just getting cranked up and was soon blowing at gale force, making my tent shudder and strain and the tent walls creak like rifle shots. Surely, the next gust would take us full sail off over the jungle unless I could prevent it. There was only one thing to do. I dug out a coil of rope and went back to see if I could reinforce the guy ropes or something. The nearest sizeable tree was awash in the breakers, but it was either get wet or stand a chance of having the tent blow down, so I floundered out into the surf and secured the rope from tree to tent frame; then back into the tent to find dry shoes, socks, and pants.

Somehow the night crept by. The tent did not blow down or wash away and no wild creatures came out of the jungle to devour us. It amused me later to think how quickly I'd forgotten the imagined menace of the jungle when faced with the more immediate danger of wind and sea. I remember spending considerable time during that long night in sober reflection on what kind of damn fool I really must be to come off into Nowhere like this to be a hermit. But, by the time the sun was up and the wind was down, I realized that nothing serious had resulted from it all, except losing a night's sleep. My courage was restored. I fixed a new fire hole, cooked some oatmeal, and then set out with machete in hand to find a new campsite.

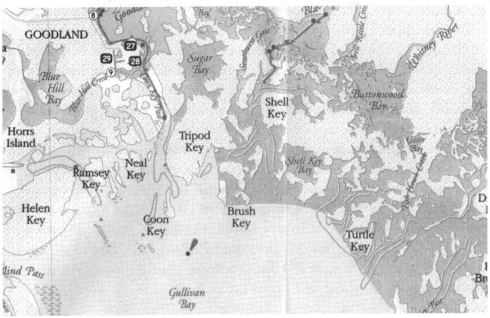

Map of Bush Key

Chapter 3

Brush Key — Aptly Named

A cloudless sky of deepest cerulean blue got together with a cool breeze to make the low-pressure system that had whipped through during the night seem only a bad dream. Responding to this bracing weather and feeling in top form despite the lack of sleep, Willie and I explored the beach side of the island all the way to the north end. This wasn't very far, actually somewhat less than 500 yards at a rough guess. The jungle that had looked so foreboding in the night turned out in daylight to be a very small, innocent looking patch that gave way on the north on higher ground and different vegetation altogether…shrubs and cactus mostly.

The beach was a disappointment. It was quite narrow and not at all the sparkling sandy beach it had appeared to be as we approached the island by boat. It was sandy in spots, but mostly made up of broken shells and fragments of which I later learned was something called "worm rock." But, I could see why we had not attempted a landing along that side. A wide mud flat was exposed at low tide that extended the entire length of the island.

I was also a trifle disappointed in not finding any coconut palms. Somehow, one thinks of life on a tropical isle in terms of coconuts and bananas. There were no nubile island maidens either. The fronds of one lone Sabal or Cabbage palm were visible above the trees back in the woods which helped a little to preserve a romantic, tropical aura.

The highest part of the island was about midway along, and it was halfway up the slope of this miniature hill that I found what I hoped would be a safe campsite. A huge dead tree was lying near the beach, and over the years it had trapped all manner of flotsam from high storm seas to form a solid barrier to the ocean. The spot I picked for my tent was far enough above it so that this barrier would not impede my view of the bay, or wouldn't after I had cleared some of the surrounding brush away. Yet, it would protect me from any but hurricane seas. There were trees enough all around to shelter the tent from wind in any direction.

With the entire day ahead of me I took plenty of time on this new campsite, clearing the brush, digging out roots, and bringing dozens of buckets of sand to level the area. There was another large tree trunk lying nearby which I earmarked for a chopping block for firewood. I dug a temporary fire hole near that and then cleared a path to the beach.

By the time that much was done, the tide was pretty well in again, nice and friendly now, so we went back to our original, ill-chosen spot and proceeded to move. The easiest way, of course, was to pile stuff in the boat and row up to the new camp. It took several trips, but beat the hell out of portaging by back.

Early in the afternoon the tent was up, right side to this time, facing the beach, and the gear stowed away. I found an old tin can that had washed ashore, used it to hold a few fiddler crabs I scouted up for bait, and went back to the little cove where I had tied my boat the night before to try my luck. Two plump sheepsheads fish were easily tempted and were soon sizzling in the skillet. To go with the fish; I boiled some rice and a pan of purslane greens and enjoyed to the fullest my first true hermit meal.

Later, after it got dark and before the moon came up, Willie and I took a walk along the beach to look at the stars. Well, anyway, I looked at the stars and believe me, they were something to see for the first time out there. With no city lights to compete and no smog to dull their brilliance, they formed a sparkling canopy of scintillating jewels stretching from the far horizon where sea and sky met, to the tips of the trees behind us. It was so quiet, you could actually feel it, as if you were in a vacuum and the sensation was of being reduced in size to a mere speck beneath the wonder of the celestial vault.

When Willie, who was having the time of his life, barked at something, I was startled to hear an echo. I gave a shout to test the effect, and it was exactly like the sound you'd get from shouting in a totally empty room. Very curious. We sort of drifted back to the tent then, buoyed by this ethereal serenity and both slept soundly and long.

During the next few days I was kept busy putting finishing touches to the camp, which was to be my home for seven months. I made a clearing in the middle of a thick clump of brush some fifty feet to one side of the area and dug a latrine. Scouting along the beach I found a couple dozen hunks of worm rock the size of my two fists, and with these I built a more-or-less permanent fireplace...more-or-less, because I discovered that the rocks had a tendency to crumble into powder after a few fires, so I was constantly replacing one here and there.

What I needed for the final cleanup was a rake, an item I had not thought to bring. But I found a tough old root about two inches thick, which at one point had grown a perfect right angle. I cut it so that there was a handle one side of the right angle and short length on the other...something like a lazy-boy grass cutter. It worked fine as a rake substitute. With it I scraped away the leaves and twigs in the front yard, leaving a couple of flowering shrubs and a cactus to give a landscaped appearance.

Later, I had the good fortune to acquire a large tarpaulin, which made a canopy over the part of the yard where I could sit in the shade of an afternoon, and enjoy a pipe or two while watching the birds, or an occasional boat out in the bay.

The tent was fairly large, measuring nine by fourteen feet with a center area high enough to walk around in and two shorter wings. The camp cot took up one wing, footlocker in number two, and various boxes of tools and canned goods were in the other. In the center there was a folding card table and camp chair. My two five-gallon containers of fresh water were near the tent door. After living in a three-bedroom, two-bath house, it seemed a trifle crowded, but it was easy to get philosophical about it. Everything I needed to sustain life was ready to hand, and what more did a guy need anyhow?

Tent campsite at Brush Key, with Willie in foreground.
(Photo courtesy of Mark Cowell)

One of the fringe benefits in becoming a hermit which had appealed to me no end during the months of planning was the alluring prospect of never again having to listen to the jangle of an alarm clock in the early morning, or having to be at work at a certain time or take orders from anybody. I had indulged in many a beatific vision of myself taking long siestas in the shade of some tropical tree, followed by a dip in the cool surf; of going fishing whenever the fishing bug bit; eating and sleeping as the spirit moved … in short, the idyllic life. But, the curious thing was that without any conscious thought on my part, I fell into a daily routine of getting up at the first blush of daylight, eating at approximately the same time each day, going to the crapper at regular times, and keeping busy-busy till dark. After dark, I would read an hour or two by candlelight and hit the sack.

Possibly, this departure from my much cherished dreams of indolence could be explained by my strict New England Yankee upbringing in which lolling about in the shade is nothing short of sinful. However, I think the more immediate reason was my insatiable curiosity. Here was an entirely new and exotic world and I couldn't gulp it in fast enough.

Obviously, one of the first major projects after the home site was in order was to explore my island. This was far from easy to do, it took several months, in fact. Starting along the beach and probing any spot that seemed to open a way into the interior, I soon discovered why the island was called "Brush Key." The undergrowth and vines were so thick that between keeping a weather eye out for snakes and trying to plow my way through the stuff, I couldn't see much of anything else. I rowed around to the lee side to see if there was any place there that would lead me inland, but that side was solid mangrove swamp. The only way to find out what was in the interior of my island was to cut trails into it, a job that kept me busy part of every day until well into the summer.

Each day I'd put on sturdy leather boots topped by snake-proof puttees and set out with shotgun, root rake and machete to hack out another fifty or hundred feet of path. After a few weeks of not seeing anything more menacing than a swamp rabbit, I left my shotgun at home; and after a month or two of not finding a snake of any description, let alone a poisonous one, I quit wearing the puttees. I kept the boots though, to protect my legs from cactus thorns.

Hacking these trails wasn't the easiest thing in the world for an alcohol soaked, overweight, middle-aged guy who has spent most of his adult life in non-physical jobs. But sore, stiff muscles soon became tough, and the flab began to melt away, and I soon felt better physically than at any time since basic training in World War II. The trail making also resulted in a growing stock of firewood since I usually dragged a load of dead branches back to the tent at the end of each day's stint.

Eventually, there was a smoothly wide path leading back into the woods directly behind my tent and following along the ridge of high ground to the north beach. Another trail branched off to skirt around the east side of this high ground close to the mangrove swamp and more or less parallel to the first. A third path led from the tent directly to the reef at the south end. My plan was to link all these together with cross trails, but I never completed the job. With the advent of the summer rainy season, the mosquitoes were so thick that even with a head net, long-sleeves, and a square of heavy tarpaulin that I fashioned to tie over my shoulders and back, it was still unbearable. All of this covering was too damn hot to wear in over 90 degree temperature, and the more I perspired, the more tempting I became to the bugs.

Like the man who went over the mountain and only saw the other side of the mountain, I didn't find anything spectacular after all my effort. No pirate treasure or Indian relics ... no skeletal remains of previous intrepid explorers. Aside from some fantastic root formations where some previous hurricane had partially uprooted a couple of huge gumbo limbo trees and the roots had gone back to earth in weird shapes, the only interesting thing I found were some mysterious holes fifty feet or more in diameter and four or five feet deep. The mystery part was that at high tide they would be partially filled with salt water despite the fact that they were located spank in the center of the island and surrounded on all sides by high ground. I could only surmise that the water seeped in through the loosely packed and porous shells and sand beneath the topsoil, but as to how they got there in the first place, I haven't the faintest idea.

Under the largest of the gumbo trees was a fairly open space that looked as if it might have been cleared at some time and there were four poles about twelve feet high stuck in the ground to form a square. It was likely a frame for a tent canopy, which would prove that I was not the first person to camp on Brush Key.

In the sinkhole, as I called it, nearest my tent I discovered a colony of giant, red-clawed fiddler crabs, some measuring up to inches in width. They were excellent bait, I found, after I learned how to pick them up without getting pinched. They could draw blood with no trouble at all.

One day when I went there to catch a few of these little monsters, I found fresh panther tracks in the mud. Reviewing the tide schedule in my mind, I knew that early in the previous evening, high tide would have caused the hole to be filled with water. The panther then must have crossed later in the night after the tide had receded. It gave me momentary goose bumps to realize that sometime during the night while Willie and I were deep in innocent sleep, a panther had actually crossed my island not a hundred yards away.

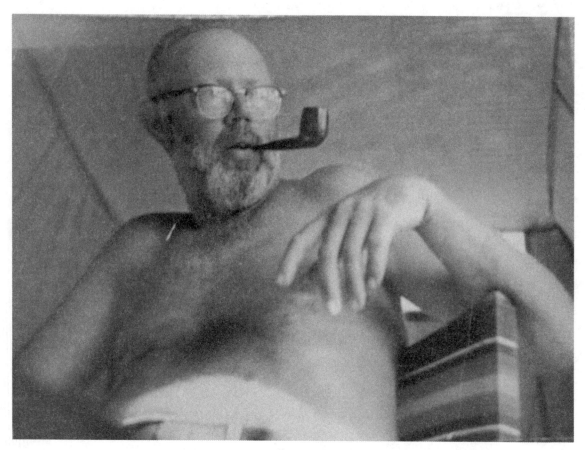

Enjoying an after-lunch pipe

photo taken by son Mark Cowell on a visit to Brush Key

Although the entire ten years I have lived the hermit life surpass any other period of my life for what you might consider as a span of sustained happiness, the first couple of months on Brush Key with all the exploring, fishing, poking around in tide pools, breathing the clean salt air, and generally basking in the wonder and beauty of unspoiled nature were beyond any doubt the nearest to perfect contentment it is humanly possible to achieve in this life. From the time of my arrival in February until the summer rains began in late May, the weather was ideal. Most days were summer warm with cool nights expressly designed for sleeping.   Exercise, simple diet, peace and quiet, and complete lack of psychological pressures of any kind soon put me in tiptop physical condition. And there were so many fascinating things to see and do that boredom was no problem, though it became so later on. All in all, I concluded that hermits were not so dumb after all.

Chapter 4

Eatin' Grass

Goodland dock near local café

On one of my trips into Goodland for mail I stepped into the local Café for a cup of coffee. The kind hearted, motherly waitress gave me a wink and a grin and said,

"You still out there eatin' grass?"

"Yup," I replied, patting my paunch, "That's what I'm a-doin'."

She considered this a minute, then said,

"It don't be hurtin' you none by the look."

What she was talking about was my self-proclaimed and appointed role as a researcher in survival foods. Looking back on it, I think I'd have been just as well off if I had told people flat out that I was planning to become a hermit. But, I guess I was self-conscious about my real reason … my drinking problem … and felt that I had to project an image that would be acceptable to everyone. I had given the postmistress[2] a spiel about doing some research in edible plants. I even went so far as to mention the University of Miami and a Government agency in a way that might suggest that I was even being sponsored in this project.

---

[2] Kappy Kirk was postmaster in Goodland, 1950 – 1984.

The news got around as I suspected it might, in a variety of garbled versions. But the dear soul in the café was the only one to boil it down and tuck it into a capsule of local idiom whereby I was soon known as the guy who was "eatin' grass" out in the islands.

Which is what I was doing too, in a manner of speaking.

Let me state here that I could have lived off the land mostly, anyway. By the time I got out there I had accumulated enough knowledge for it. I knew, for instance, that all birds were edible. All the small animals I'd be likely to encounter were edible. All shellfish in uncontaminated waters were edible. Practically all the local fish were edible, and there were over a hundred trees, shrubs, and plants in the general area, which had edible portions like leaves, shoots, roots, or fruit. I even had an understanding with Mrs. Morton whereby if I found an especially succulent-looking plant not listed in her book I could mail samples to her for analysis.

There is no doubt that anyone equipped with this much information, the necessary equipment and sufficient motivation, could sustain life out here for a long time. But I only dabbled at it, for several reasons. The primary one being that I didn't have to. Charlotte had worked out a generous plan whereby she would drive over to Goodland every couple of months or so and bring me a load of staples: coffee, sugar, flour, tobacco, and so on. The next reason was that I discovered right off that very few of the edible plants listed in Mrs. Morton's book were to be found on Brush Key or any of the surrounding islands. The majority of these plants can be found only on the mainland hammocks or along the upper reaches of the rivers that lead into the Everglades proper where there is more fresh water than salt. This is particularly true of plants like the common cattail or the Seminole Indian "coontie root" which would provide the starches basic to any diet.

The most important reason was a discovery I made about myself. I found, unhappily, that I was not made of the stuff to undertake foraging expeditions alone into these formidable hinterlands. My fears of getting lost, having motor trouble, or getting snake bitten far outweigh what small hankering I might have had for such exploration. I found it much more comfortable to hang close to home, using only the native foods that were easily available. I eventually quit even that when I found how much work was involved. Most of God's critters manage to live off the land, but you may have noticed that they don't have time for much else.

And hermits, even phony ones, have a tendency to be lazy.

But I did experiment with quite a few things and I'll tell you about some of these culinary treats.

One of the first things I noticed on Brush Key was the lush growth of sea purslane (*Sesuvium portulacastrum*) along the beach. I'll not try to describe it or any of the other plants I mention. If you are interested in sampling any of these native delicacies it would be wise to get a copy of Mrs. Morton's book or a similar, well illustrated, documented guide. Anyway, purslane is the first wild plant I tried and the one I have used most often as a green vegetable. I still eat it occasionally. It can be eaten raw or cooked, and I have used it both ways, in a salad with chopped onions, plain boiled with fish, or chopped into scrambled eggs (when I am lucky enough to have eggs). It is unusual for a green in that it is already salty. For some curious reason women seem to prefer its unique flavor more than men, a useless fact that I'll leave you to puzzle over.

When one of my trails was finally cut over the hill and down to the mangrove swamp, I discovered an equally lush growth of saltwort (*Batis maritime*). As the name implies, this is also salty, but not so much as purslane to my taste. Although this, too, can be eaten raw, I have always preferred to soften it some by boiling for ten minutes.

The next most prolific edible plant on Brush Key was cactus: both *Opuntia dillenii* and *Opuntia austrina*, which I refer to as large and small. I guess everyone knows that cactus pears are edible, but so are the joints, or pads, which again can be eaten raw or cooked.

I recall finding a large stand one day with many newly budded pads looking all fresh and juicy and bright green. I picked a dozen or so for my dinner. Obviously one had to remove the spines, which I proceeded to do by cutting them out with a jackknife. What I didn't know was that at the base of each yellow thorn is a little dark nest of the tiniest, most devilish, glass-like spicules. I made that discovery when I went to wipe my hands after getting the pads cut up in the pot and found dozens of the pesky things stuck in my fingers. I had to use a magnifying glass and tweezers to get them all out. I was not so lucky with one that got stuck under my tongue while eating the stuff. That one was impossible to see or remove no matter how I prodded, rubbed, rinsed, or cussed. It was several days before it worked out, or digested, or whatever the hell it did.

Cactus pads have a bland taste, which is to say no taste at all and a mucilaginous quality somewhat like okra only more so. But as you might have guessed they never became a staple item in my diet because of the work involved removing the dam stickers.

Toward the end of summer I got my first crop of ripe cactus pears. Like the pads, or joints, these too have several clumps of those devilish microscopic spicules. But Mrs. Morton's book described how to avoid getting stuck by splitting the fruit longitudinally and scooping out the juicy pulp with a spoon. Naturally, I tried a few that way to see if they might come somewhere near to being a delicacy. They didn't. They were insipid and full of hard round seeds. But the fruity part is the most gorgeous red color imaginable. Close to a rose madder or alizarin crimson I'd say.

Since it was obvious that I wasn't going to add these to my diet and since I was so taken with the color, I began to wonder what could be done with them. Of course! Wine. What else?! I know nothing about making wine (fortunately) but I had an idea that if you got the juice out of a good bunch of these pears and added sugar and maybe a few raisins nature would do the rest. So after a long tedious job of scooping the pulp out of dozens of pears, squeezing it through some mosquito netting in lieu of cheesecloth, adding water and sugar and so on and removing several more goddamed stickers from my fingers I got about two gallons set up and tucked into a corner of the tent to ferment. The very next day it was sort of heaving and bubbling and a scum forming on the top. Aha, Yee-ah! I might be out on an island with no money in my jeans, but by God I could tie one on anyway. What's more, I told myself gleefully, I would have an endless supply while the pear season lasted.

Two days.

Three.

By now I could smell the alcohol and feel the tingle in my nose. Terrific. Beautiful. I was already beginning to drool.

At the end of five days I couldn't resist testing it. I got a plastic tumbler and started to pour. What the hell? A thick, gloppy, viscous mass oozed out of the jug and plopped into the glass. Apparently the mucilaginous quality of the pads also permeated the fruit. Fermentation undoubtedly increased this gummy effect somehow.

After I recovered from a fit of whooping and giggling at the idea of being the first person to invent a wine you could eat with a spoon I forced myself to take a swallow of the goop anyway. Just like eating raw oysters, I swear. And of course, I had not let the fermentation be completed so there was maybe a half-percent of alcohol content.

Shit!

I pitched the mess out in the front yard where the beautiful red stain may be seen to this day for all I know.

So much for *Opuntias*.

Another plant I use from time to time is the sea rocket (*Cakile fusiformis*) that is not too plentiful hereabouts. It can be cooked and I tried it that way, but I prefer it raw in a salad. It has a sharp, piquant flavor, reminiscent of horseradish.

There were a scant half-dozen wild papaya trees on my island, so I was able to sample the small fruits when they ripened. I can say no kind words for them. They were bitter and full of seeds. There are supposed to be other edible parts to this plant, the young leaves and flowers may be cooked and eaten as greens, but when I picked a couple I found a milky sap running out of the stem, which was extremely bitter. I passed 'em up. The pithy interior of the stem and the root when boiled are also edible, but to try either of these meant destroying the whole plant, which I was unwilling to do. For the same reason I have never eaten swamp cabbage (the heart of the Sabal Palmetto) which is a well-known Florida delicacy. I used to think that my sentiment about destroying these graceful trees was foolish since everyone else came along and hacked them down willy-nilly, but in our current year with the great emphasis on ecology and conservation it seems my sentiment is justified.

There were no Spanish bayonet (*Ucca aliofolia*) plants on Brush Key but I found some nearby. They bloom in April with a pyramid cluster of white flowers at the apex of each stalk. These flowers are edible and are quite crisp and tasty. The almost microscopic yellow lice in them do not seem to affect the flavor any. The fruit is also supposed to be edible; but though the plants in this area bloom regularly year after year there is never any fruit. This mystery was eventually solved for me by Mrs. Morton who wrote that pollination of the Yucca flower is effected by a certain type of moth that apparently does not exist out here.

Once, on another island I found a long scarlet bush (*Hamelia patens*) with some attractive berries, which reminded me of good ole New England huckleberries. With pleasant anticipation I tossed a few in my mouth. What a shock! They were the bitterest of bitter. I had to spit for a Goddamned hour. I assumed, of course, that I had made an error in identification although the plant seemed to tally with the description in my book. Some time later, Mrs. Morton came out to visit me and see how I was making out. I took her to see that particular bush. She affirmed that it was indeed the *Hamelia patens*.

"I don't understand, " I said in great puzzlement, "those berries tasted awful."

"Well," she commented dryly, " I said they were edible. I didn't say that they had to taste good."

That observation could apply to many survival foods. If you were starving there are many things to be eaten for nourishment, but taste lousy as hell. Come to think of it, there aren't any of these native plants, which I would consider delicious. This is just as well, perhaps, when you consider the rapacious attitude of too many people toward nature's bounty.

The dried leaves of the Red Mangrove tree can be brewed into tea or smoked in a pipe as a tobacco substitute. I've tried both and can't rate them very highly. The tea is stimulating and has a familiar astringency, possibly from the tannic acid content, but it does suffer a bit by comparison to orange pekoe. Smoking the leaves in my pipe brought back memories of puffing corn silk behind the barn.

Since all shellfish found in clean water are edible, I sampled all the various species I could find out here. Those were the whelks, both lightning and pear, crown conchs, tulips, rose and heart cockles, sunray Venus clams, quahog clams and murex. I found them all to have two things in common, they all had a delicious seafood flavor, and they were all tough as whet-leather. Cockles and clams diced in tiny pieces in a chowder are passable, but I found the best way to utilize any of them was to run them through the meat grinder, mix with flour and cornmeal, shape into patties, season and fry. There are interesting entries in my diary like; "Today had tulip burgers, or crown burgers, whelk burgers" etc.

I've got to back up here a bit. The easiest way to get these critters out of their porcelain-hard shells is to dump them in boiling water then pry them out with a knifepoint or ice pick.

Although I imagine it wouldn't hurt anyone to eat all the crap that's there the way you eat oysters, I generally clean 'em up a bit, saving only the meaty parts.

As to the edible qualities of oysters, blue crabs, and stone crabs, nothing need be said. Oysters are always here in great profusion while the crabs come and go. It is quite possible, however, for even a hermit to indulge in frequent gourmet dining on these delicacies. Now days, I rarely indulge in the more exotic but less succulent species unless I have a guest who desires a typical hermit meal. Then I whop up some purslane and whelk burgers with sea rocket salad on the side.

Now we come to the birds that I understand are all edible though many sea birds are supposed to be have a very unpleasant, fishy flavor. I'll probably never know from my own experience as I have yet to eat a wild bird. I shot one once with the intention of eating it, but when I picked it up and pinched the thighs and breast the way my mother used to check roosters back home to see how much meat they had on them, I found this poor bird (which I later learned was a double-breasted cormorant) to be nothing but feathers, bones, and birdshot. It was extremely easy while still holding that pathetic carcass to believe that all birds would be an equal waste of bullets, particularly since shooting things is not my bag.

One more related story and I'll get on to something else. I was fishing along the reef one day when I heard Willie barking up a storm and running wildly back and forth near the roots of a huge mangrove tree that grew at the land end of the reef. The cause of his frenzy was a young raccoon safely ensconced inside the cage of roots. My first thought was: "Ah. Here's dinner." But the coon had such sad, scared eyes that a great surge of pity went through me. "What's the matter with you?" I asked myself. "Aren't you supposed to be investigating survival foods and living off the land?" "Yeah," I replied, "but the little bugger looks ..."

"Little bugger, hell! He's food, protein, meat, and according to all you've heard prime eating too."

And so it went until I finally talked myself into getting my gun. Then I began to wonder how I'd get it out of that tangle of roots if I did shoot it, so I changed my mind and decided to let it escape. I called Willie off, much to his disappointment as he was mightily interested in playing with this newfound pal. I thought when we got far enough away the coon would make a dash for the jungle. Instead, it clambered up the tree and perched in the fork of a limb some twenty feet up where it was a prime target.

Some atavistic urge drove me back to take a bead on it, but then I noticed those wide brown eyes again, staring out of the little black mask. "O.K. So I'm a chicken hermit. I'll confess it." Aside from that cormorant, and I regretted killing that since I didn't eat it, I have never shot another wild creature. I've eaten a few coons but Willie did the killing after he got big enough. He didn't seem to mind ... enjoyed it in fact.

Well, so much for enlarging the horizons of man's knowledge of survival in the wilderness. I cheated by not utilizing many of the available natural foods, but then again, I've survived for over ten years and rather well.

Willie has possum treed
(Photo courtesy of Everglades City High School students)

E. Foster Atkinson

Chapter 5

E. Foster Atkinson ... In Memoriam

One day, not long after I'd gotten settled in, I was enjoying an after-lunch pipe in the front yard when Willie suddenly went yapping down the south path. I looked up and here came a strange black dog. Then I heard a "Hallo" followed by the appearance of a slightly built, gray-bearded man sort of shuffle limping along, and a sea captain's cap perched jauntily on his head. I moseyed on down to meet him and said, "Hi." In reply the man gasped,

"Asthma---wait---I ----get m' breath."

"Come on up and sit a bit," I said.

When he had recovered his wind and could talk he introduced himself as Foster. "...and this is 'Tootsie,' he added, calling up his dog. I told him who I was and who Willie was.

"Pleased t' meetcha," he said, "-uh-uh- I – uh saw your ... uh tent th' other day on my way to town and ...uh ... then in town ... uh ... I heard there was a ... a man out here studying survival and ... uh ... I says to myself I says, 'here's my chance to learn something.'"

I grinned at thinking how effectively my propaganda in Goodland was working and said,

"Well, I don't know much about survival ... yet. All I know so far is about a few native things you can eat."

"That's more'n I know," Foster said, "but ...uh... the lady in the ... uh ... Post Office told me she thought you was ... uh... connected with the Government."

"Well, I did tell her that I had been in correspondence with a couple of Government agencies and a Mrs. Morton at the University of Miami, but ..."

"That's right," he interrupted, "she ... uh... uh... mentioned the university too."

"Anyway," I continued, "I'm really out here strictly on my own. I thought I'd see if I could live off the land but so far I haven't knuckled down to it, getting settled and all."

We yakked survival for a little while and then Foster began to tell me about himself. He lived on an island called Dismal Key, which he estimated to be about five miles from Brush Key. He had been there for ten years he told me. He was on social security now, but before that he had made his living shelling. I flapped my ears out at that, thinking it would help my long-range plans to be able to pick up a little money along the way. When I questioned him about it he seemed willing to share his knowledge and assured me that it was possible to make some money at it. Which was true. I eventually did make a little money shelling ... very little.

He had come from Maine, originally, though he didn't have to tell me that, his down-east speech and dry humor were unmistakable. He even had his beard trimmed like an old time lobster fisherman with a sea captain's cap to match. His blue eyes were sharp and clear and shrewd. I learned later that whereas he'd traveled extensively by bus and some by freight train, he'd never been to sea. But there was no doubt that his old salt disguise fit him well, somehow.

Foster Atkins and Puddin' 1960's

We were only able to swap the high spots in our respective autobiographies on that visit. The tide was dropping and he was afraid his boat would get stranded on the beach so he didn't stay long. Before he left he invited me to visit him on Dismal Key. He had many things to show me, he said, including a couple of books on camping and survival. I got out my chart and he traced a course for me to follow, but I could tell at a glance that it was hopeless for me to try to find my way through all those islands, chart or no chart. He agreed to come and pick me up in a few days and show me the way.

As we started walking slowly (in deference to his asthma) toward the south beach where he had come ashore, he whistled up his dog, which was an inappropriate move at that particular moment. When the two dogs earlier had finished the usual ass-sniffing routine, they had gone rollicking off and we paid no further attention to them. Now, we discovered them in ludicrous intimacy. Willie, despite his youth was trying frantically to prove his maleness. Tootsie was doing her utmost to be a cooperative partner.

"Damn!" Foster gasped,"—didn't know the bitch was in heat."

"Well," I said, "no need to worry this time. Willie's heart is in the right place, but the rest of him sure'n hell isn't."

When we got to the boat Foster had to rest a bit before getting launched. I said, "Hey … that's quite a boat you got there."

He just wheezed and grinned. It was what I'd call a real hermit boat. It was a homemade, square-looking affair about eight feet long by four wide that might have know paint once but was now weathered gray above the water line and festooned with green slime below. But it was heavy and sturdy enough I discovered when I helped him shove it in the water and his five-horse kicker took only a couple of pulls to start.

As they putted off across the bay, Willie and Tootsie giving last minute ship to shore love signals, or so I imagined, I was struck by the irony of the situation. Foster had come to sit at the feet of the alleged Government man, but the apparent truth was that I would probably be learning a great deal from him.

True to his word, he came for Willie and me the following week and we set off for Dismal Key.

So far, in quoting Foster I have tried to capture the extreme halting quality of his speech. It's quite hopeless. It is my guess that his mind ran along some distance ahead of his tongue and the many "ers" and "uhs" were a device, which enabled him to catch up with himself from time to time without losing his place as principal speaker. Judging that it would be as distressing to read that staggered speech as it sometimes was to listen to it, I'll henceforth record his statements in normal language and let you imagine the "uhs."

O.K.?

We're on our way from my island to his with the express purpose of his teaching me the route. "There's four or five ways of going through here," he began in the granddaddy of understatements. And he proceeded to explain at great length how I could go clockwise around an island and come out someplace or other, or go counter-clockwise and come out at the same place and so on until my addled brain refused to take it in at all.

At one point, though, something came up that gave me quite a fright when he said, "This bay we're in right now is awful shallow. At a long spring tide like we had last week the whole center of it comes out of water and …"

I flapped a frantic hand to interrupt him.

"What do you mean … a <u>Spring</u> tide like last week? This is still February. A little early for spring isn't it?"

That was apparently a real dumb-ass question and I was immediately sorry that I'd asked it because he got to laughing and then wheezing and gasping till I thought he'd pack it in for sure. But he recovered and tried to explain. He said, "Ya get seven days of spring tides on the new moon and seven more on the full moon. In between ya get seven, sometimes eight days of neap (which he pronounced 'nip') tides on the first quarter and the last quarter. The spring tides run very high and very low but the neaps don't run so high or low. Sometimes they don't change much of any and then we call em 'crazy tides.' Ya got all that?"

"Hell no," I said.

"Well 'tis a mite confusin' I guess but when we get to the house I'll show ya how to figger 'em on the calendar.

"Now over there to your left along that ridge there where the gumbo limbo trees are, that's a Calusa Indian mound. There's an old cistern up there too. We'll go up and mosey around someday."

Not seeing anything that looked like a ridge to me, I said, "Great. Sounds like fun."

I realized then as he rambled on that it was quite useless for me to try to follow his directions so I tuned him out and began looking around for myself. This was the first time I had gone in among the islands away from the Gulf and I began to savor various impressions engendered by this unique and weird area. I think the dominant feeling was one of time displacement. Had there been a mist over the islands I would not have been a bit surprised to see a dinosaur raise its slimy head among the trees or one of those prehistoric flying reptiles flap by on hissing wings. It was that kind of country.

The greenish-brown water was a mirror still reflecting the shoreline so perfectly that if you were able to travel upside down it would have looked exactly the same.

We would come through a narrow pass into a bay and in no time, looking back, the pass would have disappeared. At one point we entered what looked like a small creek between solid green walls of tall mangrove trees only to find shortly that it branched off in several directions. Like a maze. How could one ever remember which branch to follow?

In one of the larger bays several porpoises were chasing mullet in the shallow water near shore, thrashing it into a frothy boil. Everywhere smaller fish were breaking the surface with tiny circles and when a larger mullet would leap clean into the air to splash belly-down again, ole Willie would jump too and press himself against my legs for protection.

Around every bend in the circuitous route, egrets and blue or white herons wading among the mangrove roots would flap away with raucous, scolding cries.

There seemed to be no landmarks, no guideposts, and no distant objectives to determine which way to go. Many spots looked so much like ones just passed that I felt we most certainly were traveling in circles. Yet, Foster droned happily on.

But then we emerged into a bay some larger than all the others and at the far side in the direction we were heading there was a definite point of land.

"That," said Foster, bringing me out of my reverie, "is the best island of all. I named it myself … Foster Key …and now," he continued as we swung by this island, "if you see a dock around the next bend we ain't lost."

We weren't lost.

As we approached the rickety dock I got my first glimpse of his house perched on the top of a little hill, little guessing that it would someday be my home too. What it reminded me of with it's sway backed and unpainted boards weathered to a silver gray, was a picture I'd seen of New England farm houses built back in colonial times. I don't know what I'd expected exactly but after threading through the seemingly endless labyrinth of ancient waterways and then to come upon a house out of a history book … it was a bit of a shock to me to say the least.

I asked him how old it was. "It's not awful old," he said. "Fella that built it back mebbe forty, fifty years had a little farm here. Pigs, chickens and a garden."

"Way out here?" I exclaimed.

"This ain't much more'n seven … eight miles from town … as the crow flies."

"Yeah … the crow," I said, thinking vaguely of a big black bird banking around islands and costing down shady channels. I asked him, then if he owned it.

"No. I guess I'm just what you might call a caretaker. I'll tell ya the story sometime how I happened to come here."

Conversation ceased at this point because in hauling his boat up on shore and tying it to a tree he had run out of breath again: and toiling up the path to the house didn't help any. At the front porch we paused until he got his speaking wind back. Then with a flourish he said,

"Here she is. My two-bedroom, split level, waterfront home. Come on in."

It was like stepping into a combined museum and library but at the same time unmistakably a hermit's lair. No feminine touches visible. Hundreds of paperback books lined shelves along two walls; others were piled here and there along with many old magazines and papers. Another shelf was loaded with curios such as a baby octopus in a jar of alcohol, a set of shark's teeth, freak starfish and various seashells. The head and pelt of a wildcat hung on another wall. This main room was large. There were three single beds in it, two or three chairs, including an armchair recliner, a dinette set, even an old TV with a colored picture pasted on the video tube. Near his bed was a small shelf with a contraption of wires and electronic components, which he told me was a diode radio that he had made.

"Plays all the time. No batteries to wear out," he said, handing me an earplug to try. Sure enough, I could hear faint music when I stuck it in my ear.

"Electronics is one of my hobbies," he explained, leading down two steps to the lower level, which contained his kitchen, workshop and a spare bed. "That's how come I got the TV set. Fella brought it out to me so's I could tear the innards out for wires and transistors and such."

By this time my mind was sufficiently blunted by the impact of so many inconsistencies that the idea of having electronics as a hobby miles from the nearest electric power source seemed perfectly natural.

Seeing a refrigerator in the kitchen didn't rock me too badly either but enough so I had to ask him if it worked.

"Sure it works," he beamed. "Bottled gas."

In the third room, which was a combination bedroom and storeroom there were three double-decker bunks.

"Why so many beds?" I asked.

"Well, the fellas that own this place used to bring whole gangs of people with 'em when they came down to fish, but now they've built another cabin on the other side of Dismal so this room don't get used much anymore." When he had completed the tour he asked me,

"What do you think of it? Not bad for an old hermit."

"It's unbelievable," I said honestly.

He then started bringing things to show me: baskets woven from sea oat grass, a ball of twine he had made from the fibers of the Spanish bayonet plant, a ceramic ashtray made of a sort of clay he had dug from a pit on the island, a hand loom for weaving and samples of things he had made with it. It was easy to see that time had never hung heavily on his hands. When I said something to that effect, he said,

"Hobbies. Got all kinds of hobbies. I get all fired up on one and work on it day and night for awhile until I get sick of it. Then I start on another. Eventually, I get back to the first one and make the rounds again. Always looking for new ones too."

For supper he fixed macaroni and cheese from a package and made some surprisingly fluffy biscuits in a skillet, followed by a piece of homemade raisin pie. I wanted to know if I could make biscuits like that over an open fire and he gave me the recipe. From that, and by adding cornmeal and making a change or two, I eventually developed my so-called Skillet Bread, which I'll say more about later on.

When it got dark he lighted his kerosene lamp and we sat long into the night, smoking and swapping yarns. One of his stories concerned a memorable drunk he had been on out in San Francisco or somewhere and had fallen down some cement stairs breaking his metatarsal arch which accounted for his limp and the fact that he could never wear ordinary shoes; only those damn toe-busting, thong-type sandals known as Zoris. This led to his admitting that he was an alcoholic too. An entirely different breed, though. He was a bar drunk as opposed to my solitary, bedroom drinking.

During the remaining years of his life we visited back and forth quite often. Usually an overnight visit … sometimes longer. I believe that he told me everything that had ever happened to him during his rather sad life … not once, but time after time. I'm sure I must have bored him with all of my personal anecdotes as well.

It got to be a helluva drag toward the end. Because of his breathing difficulties he never moved around much and consequently he needed very little sleep. I could no long stay with him, going to sleep in spite of myself. One night he was doing a repeat of some incident in his second marriage, which I knew was good for an hour or two at least. I flopped around a couple of times in my bunk and heaved a big sigh and shortly gave out with an imitation snore. He stopped his "uh-uh-uh" recital and said,

"You awake?"

No Answer.

"Hey, Al."

No answer.

"Well God dam. He's gone to sleep on me again."

~

Foster died in April of 1972 which means that for the first five years I had a good friend and neighbor to help me get used to the various aspects of living my pseudo-hermit's life.

For the first couple of years that I knew him he insisted that his extreme breathing difficulties were due to asthma, which he said he had suffered from off and on most of his life. Later, he became convinced that it was not asthma at all, but emphysema. I could write a whole chapter on the patent and other nostrums he tried, and the many truly pitiful attempts he made to quit smoking cigarettes.

During his last Christmas season he went into Goodland to get his mail and on the way back ran onto an oyster reef and busted the lower unit in his old motor. He had to row the remaining six miles to get home, which was a miraculous feat for an old man with emphysema who couldn't walk from the dock to his house without stopping once or twice to get his wind. But it was also the beginning of the end. The next day he had lost his voice and could only whisper. We both assumed that from his exposure to a cold night on the water he had gotten a touch of bronchitis or something. But when, after a couple of weeks and much varied medication his voice had not returned, it was apparent that something more serious was involved.

Like me, he was not a true hermit, meaning that he had lots of company too. One of his frequent visitors was a retired doctor who tried every persuasion that he could think of to get Foster to go to a hospital, for treatment. I was visiting Foster one day when the doctor came by and I heard him tell Foster,

"If you don't get some help for that condition of yours, you are going to die!"

"Ayuh," Foster whispered, "Mebbe I am, but the way I see it, the Bible says a man has threescore and ten years to live and I'm over that now … livin' on borrowed time. I guess my number is up that's all."

He got steadily weaker after that. Barely able to walk around the house and do for himself. In fact he didn't do for himself well enough. He ate less and less, and this of course, weakened him still more.

During his last few days he knew he was close to the end and kept a diary of his symptoms. The doctor I referred to was the one who found his body and from its position on the floor he was apparently trying to get from his bed to his favorite chair at the table. The doctor estimated that he had only been dead for a day or two, which was fortunate as far as his dog, was concerned. It was hungry but not starved and as far as I know is still leading a happy life with Foster's grandchildren.

There are two bright spots in this macabre picture. Foster was cheerful and apparently not too uncomfortable right to the end. And he had his heart's desire to die on Dismal Key. He wanted to be buried on Dismal, too, but there were legal complications forbidding it. I like to think that the poor old guy never knew he was buried elsewhere.

The reason I have taken the trouble to write about Foster and tell of his passing is that I am now living in the very house where he died. Also, I am now the only surviving hermit in the islands and my years are peeling off ever more rapidly. I wonder if I will be able to meet my end as peacefully and cheerfully as he did.

Foster Atkinson Oct 1969 (Courtesy of Bob Steele)

Chapter 6

Bugs 'n Things

Looking back, I would say that the seven months I stayed on Brush Key slipped by very rapidly and were exciting and happy times. Yet, the curious thing is that when I check my diary for that period I discover that nevertheless I was occasionally depressed and not at all sure that becoming a hermit was the right thing for me after all. The only way I can account for these transitory moods is to assume that adjusting to a totally different solitary way of living was sure to be accompanied by a few psychological twinges. I suppose there is also a good possibility that a modicum of homesickness was part of the syndrome.

Under the best of circumstances daily living is never wholly serene and most people will probably agree that it is better so: heat and cold, sweet and sour, yin and yang, and all that stuff. So even on my paradise island I always had a few small troubles to balance out the many good aspects.

My little outboard motor shortly became a pain in the ass, particularly since I became aware that I had been penny wise and dollar foolish in buying an off-brand motor in the first place. Furthermore, I was abysmally ignorant about the function of any kind of motor and hadn't the faintest notion of what to do to make it run. Either it did or it didn't.

No. It was even more ornery than that.

Rather than stand in the water behind the damn thing, I found a limb of a tree near the beach where I could hang it at a suitable height. Time and again I could get it buzzing good on the limb but the minute I put it back on the boat it would stay deader than a week-old corpse.

On top of that I could never get the motor and the weather to synchronize. It was necessary for me to go into town every week or so to replenish my supply of fresh water, but these trips could only be made on days when the breeze was absolutely minimal. Brush Key faced the open Gulf of Mexico and there was a bay to the north some three quarters of a mile in width that had to be crossed before I could get into the protected waters of Goodland Channel. It might sound ridiculous, but a wind of as little as ten to fifteen knots was sufficient to whip up the water enough to make the crossing in a ten- foot Jon boat hairy, if not actually dangerous. On the nice calm days I could never get the stupid motor to run. More than once I had to get on the oars and row the six-mile round trip.

Once in a great while when the weather was suitable and I would succeed in getting the motor perking and head for town; the porpoises would bug me. They were very partial to that little coffee-grinder engine, and every time they heard me popping up the channel at three miles an hour, they'd crowd around for a little game of hide and seek. Yeah, I know they are very friendly animals, and playful, and beautiful. They are also four or five feet long and probably weigh over a hundred pounds and when four or five of them began diving under my tiny boat and leaping alongside close enough to touch, I always expected to be rocked once too often and capsize. I admit, albeit reluctantly that they must be as intelligent as they are given credit for being because never once did they do more than scare the bejesus out of me.

My diary also mentions that I was having difficulty catching fish, which is true enough. I remember that daily disappointment. But there were two things I didn't take into consideration when writing up my blues back then, I did not stop to think that the publicity I'd seen touting the Ten Thousand Islands as a "fisherman's paradise" was probably no more factual than most travel copy, nor did I consider that fish come and go with different seasons and to some extent are affected by tides and phases of the moon and so on. However, as you will see in my erudite chapter on fishing, it didn't help a whole hell of a lot to learn about these peculiarities of fish behavior.

Mosquitoes

The things that bugged me most (pun intended) were the bugs. Mosquito season out here starts with the onset of the summer rains in late May or early June and continues until the first cold snap in November or December. I can only say that it's a good thing I started my adventures in February before the mosquitoes arrived or I should surely have packed it in and gone back to civilization. As it was I had adjusted well enough to my new condition by May to be able to cope with the bugs after a fashion.

I have talked to people who have described the quantity and ferocity of mosquitoes in other parts of the world, like the far north or the bayou country, and possibly my Brush Key mosquitoes could not honestly be said to be more blood thirsty than any others, but I'll stack my mosquitoes against any others anywhere on the basis of intelligence and shrewdness. These mosquitoes are highly organized.

A few examples: while a few dozen buzz around your face in a distracting maneuver, another squad or two moves in for the kill on your shoulders, ass, ankles, or wherever they can find skin or clothing they can penetrate. They are highly skilled in guerilla tactics hiding in the brush close to wherever you happen to be going, ready to ambush you in a vicious, stinging cloud. If you step into the wind figuring they'll be blown away, they simply stay around on the lee side of you. They have scouts constantly hunting tiny holes or rips in the tent through which the main battalion can enter during the night. When you douse the interior with aerosol spray the damn little buggers know enough to hide under things so they won't be affected. They even have their equivalent of kamikaze pilots, individuals which sacrifice their lives by flying directly into your mouth and nostrils so that while you are busy hawking and spitting or reaming out your nose, you're open to attack on all sides. The only consolation … and it's a small one at that … is that after you have sustained a few thousand bites, you develop immunity to their poison so that you don't swell and itch too much.

I've tried all different repellants, including some stinking shark liver oil Foster made as a survival measure. They all work to some degree but when asked what I do about mosquitoes I always say that the most effective thing is not to bathe very often. Mosquitoes dearly love a freshly scrubbed, deodorized body.

No-see-ums

The sand flies, or sand fleas (take your choice) are something else again. They are so tiny they are practically invisible, often being referred to as "no-see-ums." But can they bite! How anything that small can inflict such a sharp sting is beyond my comprehension. And they've got it over the mosquitoes by being able to penetrate ordinary screening and even mosquito netting. Like mosquitoes they have their own brand of super knowledge, being able without hesitation to land on the softest, most sensitive skin like your eyelids or the inside of your ears. They also, I think, possess a truly fantastic power. I don't know what you'd call it, some kind of black magic, maybe. I have never told any living soul about this before for fear of being considered off my rocker, or around the bend as the British say. As a result of this reticence I haven't compared notes with anyone so the experience is uniquely my own. Maybe it is really malfunction of my own nervous system that has nothing to do with the sand flies whatsoever. What happens is this … say one sand fly (though they never bite in ones) bites me just below my elbow on the inside of my forearm. I will feel the sharp sting anywhere within a one-inch radius of where the pesky thing is actually stinging me. If I then bore a finger down on the point of pain I don't squash the fly at all which continues drilling peacefully into my epidermis. How they can bite you in one spot and make it hurt in another place is totally beyond me, unless, as I said, my nerve endings are coming unglued. You can imagine the confusion when a swarm of several hundred go to work on me at the same time.

Sand flies are most active only in the early morning and at sunset except on full-moon nights when they take advantage of the extra brightness to stay busy the whole night through. A breeze will keep them away. Or a smudge. Among the many survival tricks Foster taught me early on was how to find what he called "punk wood." This is old, rotten wood that is soft enough so you can crumble it between your finger and thumb. When dry, it will smolder slowly and for some reason the smoke is not irritating to your eyes and nose like green wood smoke. It is very effective in keeping both sand flies and mosquitoes at bay. Before the first summer was gone the inside of my tent smelled like a Georgia smokehouse, my clothes like the remnants from a fire sale not to mention how the unwashed occupant of those clothes smelled.

Since I am on the subject of smoke versus bugs, this would be an appropriate time to tell you how I managed my cooking chores while on Brush Key, all over an open fire to begin with. I mentioned building a fireplace with hunks of worm-rock. It was essentially a horseshoe shaped hole in the ground lined with rock on three sides with the rock wall extending some six or eight inches above the ground level.

I left one side open for draught purposes and to provide easy access for shoveling out the ashes. My two iron straps rested crosswise at the top on which I could position my skillet and pots for cooking. This arrangement made for a safely contained fire, but it was hell to cook on because I always had to stoop, squat, or kneel to get down to it. It was good for my figure, no doubt.

My customary eating schedule in those days was coffee in the early morning, breakfast of oatmeal, corn meal mush, soup, or warmed over fish at around eleven a.m., then dinner my main or big meal at around three in the afternoon, with a snack of skillet bread and peanut butter before going to bed.

Anyone who has done any extensive cooking over an open fire knows full well what a nuisance the smoke can be. One always has to move this way or that to avoid runny eyes and coughing. But my situation where the sand flies were at their worst in the early morning, it was just the opposite. I had to keep jumping around to keep <u>in</u> the smoke … coughing and runny eyes notwithstanding. That is the reason I did my extensive cooking early in the afternoon. Any later and the mosquitoes and sand flies would have made it pure hell, smoke or no smoke.

Al cooking Skillet Bread over the open fire.
(Photo courtesy of Mark Cowell)

I have already promised to say more about my Skillet Bread and I see I have just mentioned it again, so I'll digress long enough to run that by. It's really nothing original with me. It is a close relative of bannock bread, hoe-cake or any number of easy to fix bread stuffs. My own recipe is to take equal amounts of flour and cornmeal, say a half a cup of each, a pinch of salt and a little water. I moisten the dough just enough to form it into a flattish loaf, toss it into a greased skillet, brown it on one side, flip it over and brown the other. Slow heat, if possible, so it will cook through. That's it. Later, after I got more civilized, I found that adding a touch of cooking oil to the dough helped make it a lighter in texture. Oh, I either used self-rising flour or added baking powder. Anyway, skillet bread is cheap, easy to do, and a fine sticker-to-the-ribs.

One final comment, getting back to smoke versus bugs. According to certain magazine ads my brand of pipe tobacco is supposed to be irresistible to women and bring them eager and panting to my bed. My personal experience has been that women coming within the orbit of my wreathed smoke generally only make wry faces and snide remarks about my "smelly old pipe." But one thing is for sure, my brand of tobacco is certainly pleasing to mosquitoes and sand flies.

My tent had screen cloth or mosquito netting windows and door, the door having a zipper opening. Then there were canvas tie down flaps to cover both windows and doors. The door flap when fastened to two upright aluminum rods formed an awning. Fortunately, I got a few lengths of mosquito netting and by pinning these to the sides and front of the awning with safety pins and letting them drape to the ground I made for myself a comparatively bug-snug room in which to sit and read or enjoy my meals.

Foster often said that to be a successful hermit you have to earn your "MM" degree (Master Of Makeshift). That screened-in affair I just described came close to qualifying me for my makeshift degree … but not close enough. The main fault with it was that nearly every afternoon a thunderstorm would roll my way and I'd have to unpin seventy odd safety pins, untie guy ropes, get the flaps down all around and generally batten down for a heavy rain.

There was once a rundown on the radio about the usual summer weather pattern in this area. If my memory serves it went something as follows:

"The fierce tropical sun beating down on the ever wet Everglades vaporizes great quantities of moisture which then rises to a height of several thousand feet where it forms heavy storm clouds. The cooler air over the Gulf waters begins about noontime to flow eastward into the 'Glades to fill the vacuum caused by this evaporation thus setting up the afternoon sea breeze."

Since the prevailing winds are from east to west you get a goofy situation in which the upper air is going one way and the air near the surface going in the opposite way. The upper storm clouds drift westward toward the beach nearly every day but because of the schizophrenic nature of the wind currents, one can never be sure whether the great black clouds and artillery rumble of thunder will result in a rain storm or just break up and drift away. Many a time I have dashed frantically around getting set for a deluge and nary a drop would fall. Once in awhile the force of the opposing winds would become equalized and a real ball buster of a storm pyrotechnics, deluge and all, would sit on top of me for hours. Even less frequently a change of wind direction would bring the daily storm from a more northerly quarter and I'd be fairly certain the winds wouldn't be driving the rain into the tent. Then, by leaving the door flap up and placing a thirty-five gallon galvanized garbage can (clean) under the front of it, I could catch the rainwater. During a heavy downpour my Jon boat would collect many gallons of water, too so during the summers I always have enough fresh water for drinking, dishes, laundry, and an occasional bathe.

Turtles

Although it is generally know that during June and July the mammoth loggerhead turtles come ashore on Florida beaches to lay their eggs, I was not prepared for my first turtle on Brush Key. I forgot about them, I suppose. Anyway, one night I heard a slow but steady splat-splat-splat out on the mud flats and Willie went into a frenzy of barking. I felt the crawlies on my spine. I had heard no boat but I was certain that it was the sound of heavy and ponderous footsteps, which conjured up the vision of some green-slimed zombie plodding right up out of the briny deep all draped in seaweed. I grabbed my spotlight and shotgun and went out to investigate. It was footsteps all right, but not human. A huge loggerhead turtle was slapping painfully but steadily across the flats completely ignoring Willie's frantic dashing about and yelping. I remembered then that this was the annual egg laying season and sure enough this ugly two hundred pound or so lady with her barnacle and weed encrusted shell was plodding to shore to do just that.

Undeterred by our curious watching, she heaved her awkward bulk up on the sandy beach with great stertorous breaths and wheezes, and proceeded to dig a hole with her flippers. I recall being intrigued by the fact that she used her right rear flipper to dig and the left to pat the hole smooth as she worked. So you suppose there is such a thing as a left-flippered turtle? It certainly appeared to be a very difficult and uncomfortable procedure and something that looked like tears kept oozing from her impassive eyes.

It is a terrible thing to quit the story at this point and not describe exactly how the old lady actually deposited her eggs. The truth of the matter is that the mosquitoes, having caught me out of doors at night with no repellant, had moved in for the feast of the year, calling all their cousins twice removed, and even their illegitimate offspring to the banquet.

I thought I could tough it out long enough to see the end of the show, but I couldn't. While squirming and scratching back in the tent I consoled myself with telling Willie, "So what's the big deal about laying an egg? Chickens do it every day," and other remarkable statements.

On the morning of June fifteenth I witnessed a new and awe inspiring sight. Instead of the usual crystal clear air and sparkling sea and sky, there was a light haze in the atmosphere with completely obliterated the horizon line at sea. The sky was perfectly cloudless and the haze had softened the colors in such a manner that sea and sky became one continuous shimmer of light. The effect produced by this phenomenon was to make it seem as if the edge of the shore where I stood was the absolute edge of the world. Talk about blowing your mind or however the acid heads say it! I was compelled to take a step or two backward so strong was the sensation of falling and despite my efforts to consider it rationally, the vertigo persisted until I walked away.

Later in the day I realized that it was the official opening day of the hurricane season and the shivers hit me again as I wondered if the phenomenon I had just seen was a sign and a portent of disaster to come. It wasn't, but it did get me to thinking about what to do if a hurricane should come my way. My first impulse was to abandon my hermitage and go back to civilization. This didn't altogether suit me. It was not only a matter of pride to assume that I could survive anything that nature could throw my way, but it also occurred to me that I might go back for several months only to find that no hurricanes would have remotely threatened the area.

As a matter of fact, since no feasible survival plan sprang readily to mind, I kept putting it off from day to day. I kept listening faithfully to the weather reports but all remained serene in the Caribbean. June drifted into oblivion, then July, and the sum total of my planning was to select a huge gumbo limbo tree back in the woods that had a sort of three way fork in the trunk about twelve feet from the ground. I figured that if necessary I could lash a few cross pieces up there to make and make a rough platform where I could tie down my folded tent and footlocker, then Willie and I could rope ourselves to the trunk and hope for the best. A pretty dumb plan, I admit.

What eventually happened was that Foster came to visit one day and asked me what plans I had made for a hurricane. He was not at all impressed with my platform in the tree idea, telling me that gumbos are not too sturdy in a high wind. Instead, he insisted that I should move my camp to Dismal Key where the ground was at least sixteen feet above sea level and in the event of a storm I could store my gear under his house and move in with him until it was over.

So on August 7th, the same charter boat captain who had brought me to Brush Key originally came and moved me to Dismal Key. I didn't know it at the time, but I was leaving Brush Key for good. I have since speculated that with the population growth of South Florida the next resident there may live in a high rise-condominium.

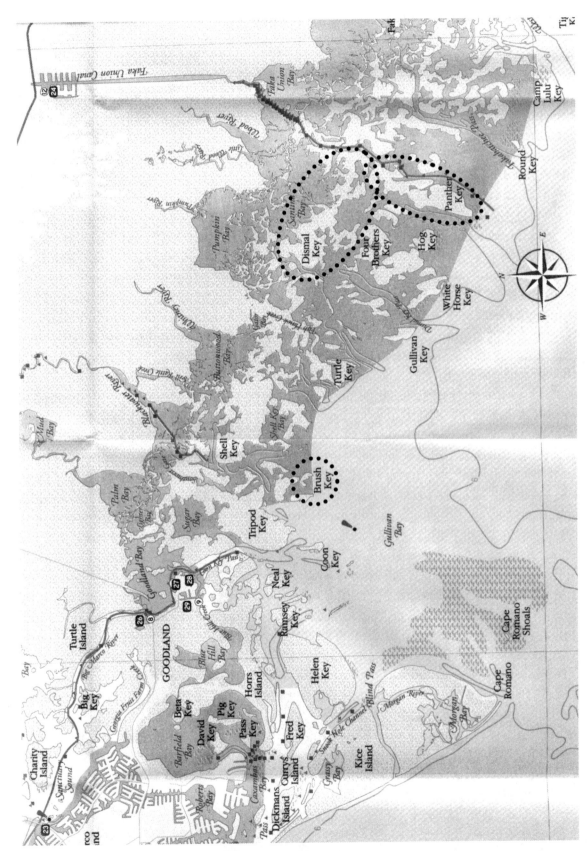

Brush to Panther via Dismal

Chapter 7

Brush to Panther via Dismal

During the three months of the 1967 hurricane season that I spent on Dismal Key the most exciting thing for me was exploring the island and learning about its history. However, I am going to skip all that for now because, as you will see, I moved back there after Foster died in 1972 and I think it will be less confusing if I put all the Dismal stories into one package.

There were only a couple of other things that happened during this interval worth recounting. Not even two. More like one and a half. The half concerns Foster's dog "Tootsie" and my "Willie." Enough months had passed since Foster's first visit to my encampment on Brush Key so that Willie was now old enough and big enough. And Tootsie had come full cycle and was in heat again. Consequently, the two dogs celebrated this happy combination of circumstances by having one helluva canine copulation.

This may not even be half a story, but I've got to put it in because you see it is the only way I can get a little sex into this book, which I understand is absolutely essential these days. Anyway, the mating was not without its somewhat wry aftermath. Willie finally came dragging his ass into my tent with his tongue lolling out half a foot and flopped on the floor so hard he practically bounced. I proceeded to fix his dinner, giving him an extra ration of meat so that he could get his strength back. He looked at his dish when I put it down for him and didn't budge. I coaxed him to come and get it. No response but a soulful look and a slight drool. I then shoved it under his nose and you should have seen the sonofagun eat as I turned the dish from time to time so he could reach it all while still lying down. And he didn't get up again until the next morning. Only when Tootsie gave birth to (no kidding) ten puppies in due time did I begin to appreciate the unstinting enthusiasm Willie had given to his part in the matter. So much for sex.

The other event has a greater import because it was one of the few times during my life as a hermit that I have had a brush with danger.

Foster and I were going into town one day in his little homemade boat. We were crossing a very shallow bay. It was so shallow that he had me peering over the bow to watch for oyster clumps or sunken logs. Which is probably why I didn't see it coming. All of a sudden we felt a tremendous jolt. Pow! The boat was lifted clean out of the water for an instant as a ten-foot shark rocketed under us. For a second or two we were both frozen with terror at the same thought. What if that monster hadn't timed his crossing to the split second and had been cut by the propeller. They say there is no way to predict what a shark will do under any circumstances, but it is quite possible that if it had been injured by the prop, it would have attacked us, and I fancy it would have made matchwood of the boat and mincemeat of us in that case. It was certainly large enough.

I think it was more of a shock to me than it was to Foster because until that time I hadn't given a thought to sharks … didn't know there were any around for that matter. Foster told me that big sharks were common in these waters, and I have seen many since then. Needless to say, my carefree swimming days ended right there.

On that same trip we passed my old campsite on Brush Key. I remember thinking how nice it would be to get back there. I had already come to think of it as home. Foster dashed this pleasant dream by calling my attention to a sign nailed to a tree nearby in plain sight. NO TRESPASSING. We found another at the north end of the island. In my best uncouth manner I shouted, "Shit!" Foster tendered expressions of sympathy.

I knew how that complication had come about. Months earlier I had been discussing with Foster my plans to remain in the Islands permanently if possible and he had suggested that I might obtain a lease on Brush Key. It was the understanding at the time that such a lease would only cost something like twenty-five dollars a year. I wrote to the land development company, which owns most of the area to inquire. They replied promptly offering me a lease on a small campsite only for one hundred dollars per year. Since I didn't have any hundred dollars and since I had worded my letter as if I were contemplating camping on Brush Key rather than that I was already there, I decided to ignore the whole matter and see what happened.

Well that's what happened. "No Trespassing." They apparently found out that I was in fact already camping there but were kind enough not to evict me. However, as soon as I had removed myself to Dismal, they hastened to let me know via the signs that I could not return without paying.

This was truly a helluva note.

I couldn't stay too long on Dismal Key with Foster. He didn't come right out and say that I couldn't, but in his shrewd fashion he had given me the word by telling me about his brother. It went something like this:

"Once m'brother Bill came to visit me," he said, "and after three, four weeks he started makin' some plans to put in a garden and raise some chickens. I says, 'Bill,' I says, 'if you wanta have a garden and all you go right ahead, but I'm givin' ya fair notice I'm leavin'. Ain't room enough here for two people permanent.'"

I got the message.

But, if I couldn't go back to Brush Key or stay on Dismal, what the hell could I do?

For the next few weeks we pawed over a half-dozen plans, none of which were feasible or desirable. Only one seemed remotely possible, though in retrospect it is nothing short of ridiculous. You recall that when Foster was showing me the route from Brush Key to his island, we were going through a bay and he called my attention to an Indian mound, which he said we'd explore sometime? That island also belongs to the same development company, but we found when we took an afternoon to look it over that at the foot of the mound was a hidden bay. It was so well hidden that if you didn't know where to find the break in the mangroves that led into it, you could pass within twenty yards and not see it. At the top of the mound was an old cistern, a large one, maybe six feet by ten. I figured that if I could clean it out, get some boards to roof it over and a ladder to climb down into it, I would have a tiny, snug dwelling secure from hurricane winds and high water. By using the hidden bay to come and go I could probably stay there a long, long time before anyone got wise to it. Still, it didn't really appeal to me, with the illegal aspect of it and all.

As it turned out, fate took a hand in things and I didn't have to give the cistern house anymore consideration. There were several key lime trees on Dismal in those days and Foster was always more than willing for anyone to come and help themselves to the fruit which would just go to rot otherwise. When a couple of guys came along one day to see of the limes were ripe, Foster introduced them to me and we got to yakking about my problem of finding a place to live now that hurricane season was about over. One of them a guy named Dick …offered to let me stay in a shack he had built on Panther Key for fishing weekends. He told me that he had been having trouble with vandals tearing it up and leaving messes of spoiled food and beer cans and junk and that he was considering building a new place nearer to Everglades City. I thanked him, but said I had some doubts about it because Panther Key is some twelve miles from Goodland and that is a bit far for an untrustworthy three-and-one-half horse motor.

"Well, you're welcome to use it anytime if you change your mind," he assured me.

Panther Key

A few days after that Foster offered to take me over to Panther saying that I should at least look at it before making up my mind. I agreed. I'm glad I did because I went for it the minute I saw it. Not that it was anything more than a rough shack built up on stilts. It was tucked cozily back in the mangroves and just to one side of it was an inlet leading to a tiny, picturesque cove that struck me immediately as a safe anchorage for my boat. The shack was also equipped with two fifty-five gallon drums placed on a rack near the entrance in such a way as to catch the rain water running off the roof. These were also connected to a plastic pipe arrangement leading into the shack to a sink where by gravity one had running water.

The interior of the shack was as Dick had implied, an indescribable mess. It looked as if in addition to being the scene of many drunken orgies it had also known a pillow fight or two. Feathers were everywhere, impeded in the screens by hundreds and in layers on the bunks and floor. Add dead roaches and rat droppings and the place could not have looked more unlivable. But the table and chairs and double bunks were all solid as was the shack itself. No leaks in the roof. Screens intact. And it could be cleaned.

I was not only taken with the shack, which at worst would be an improvement over my tent, but when I saw the beautiful beach extending for half or three quarters of a mile or more out to the open Gulf, I knew I wanted to live there. Which I did … for the next five years.

There was still the problem of my little boat, but Foster suggested that we could work out some deal about going to town in his boat, or that he could bring mail to me and so on. Which is how it started out until I was able to get a better boat.

The move to Panther Key was accomplished piecemeal over a period of several days. The first trip or two I took nothing but a broom, some rags and cleansing powder. It was a bitch of a job getting that shack fit to live in I'll tell you. I never did get all of the pin feathers out of the screens since the only way they would come out was to picked out one by one.

The third trip I took some basics: coffee, sugar, bedding and an old-timey kerosene lamp Foster had given me. From then on I lived on Panther and made daily trips to Dismal until I had the rest of my gear transported.

When I finally got settled in, I realized that I was coming up in the world for a hermit. The bunk was a great improvement in comfort over my camp cot. Actually it was a double bunk, upper and lower, so that I could now entertain an overnight guest if I wished. The two water drums when full held over a hundred gallons of clean rain water. I no longer had to worry about going to town every week to replenish my drinking supply. The running water in the sink made it possible to wash my dishes right in the shack instead of lugging them down to the beach to wash with sand and salt water. During my stay on Dismal I had made another acquisition … a little Swedish single-burner kerosene stove. My days of open-fire and smudge cooking were at an end. The kerosene lamp was, of course, much easier to read by than candles.

I now found myself proving the old cliché that the more you get the more you want. The latrine arrangement I had used for months on Brush Key was no longer satisfactory. I proceeded to design and build a better one and this achievement I modestly state, qualified me at last for my "Master of Makeshift" degree. After studying the terrain in the back of the shack I found a spot I thought might do for this new scheme and dug a hole. As I suspected, I hit salt water about three feet down. Then I knocked the bottom out of a large galvanized garbage can and placed that in the hole, snuggin' the dirt back in all around it until it was firmly planted. Over the can went a frame made from mangrove sticks to which an old toilet seat was attached for comfortable sitting. With four tall mangrove poles and some crosspieces lashed together with nylon cord since I had not nails, I constructed the outhouse frame, which was then covered on top and three sides with tarpaper from a roll someone had left under the shack. On the fourth side I hung a panel of mosquito netting to serve as a door. But the clever part was a ditch that led from the bottom of the garbage can far enough out toward the lagoon so that at every high tide ocean water would run into the crapper and out again as the tide receded, making it a self-flushing toilet. The only drawback to it was that despite the mosquito-netting door, my genuine-type mosquitoes always managed to get in. One could hardly spend any time at all in meditation without sustaining a dozen stings on that particular part of the anatomy, which is generally exposed in this most salutary attitude.

Once when Charlotte was visiting me she proceeded to use this unique accommodation. Suddenly, her cries and shrieks ripped the air for miles around. By the time I rushed out of the shack and down the path, she was emerging from the outhouse, clutching her unbuttoned slacks to keep them from falling.

"What's the matter?" I cried.

"Something was crawling on me," she wailed, indicating her rear that was still twitching from the fright of it.

"Did you get stung?" I asked, thinking of scorpions.

"I don't think so," she said.

I went in to investigate and found several wharf or tree crabs crawling around on the framework for the toilet seat. No doubt one of these had taken a stroll across the pink expanse of her fanny. They are ugly-looking little monsters about the size of a postage stamp. But they are entirely harmless. I caught one and brought it out to show her.

"See," I soothed her, "it wouldn't hurt a flea."

She wasn't entirely mollified for which I can hardly blame her. I can't say that I'd be overjoyed to have one crawling around my bare ass either.

One other thing I wanted which Charlotte was able to get for me was an old oil drum and some lengths of stove pipe with which I was able to knock together a nifty little wood burning stove.

You might wonder why anyone in subtropical Florida would ever need a heater. Let me assure you that it gets cold down here in the winter. Not like up north maybe, but plenty damn cold enough, especially for anyone who has lived here for any length of time and gotten accustomed to the tropical climate. Twenty-seven degrees F. was the coldest I ever recorded on Panther Key, but the upper thirties and low forties are not unusual during winter nights with daytime temperatures ranging between sixty and seventy. A heater is a handy thing to have around.

I had hardly gotten comfortably settled before I started having visitors. Foster came over frequently, of course, giving me a crash course in the colorful history of Panther Key which I'll get to shortly. But in addition to him, especially during that first December and January I had people wandering the beach to look at my shack nearly every day.

I didn't realize it at the time, though I might have guessed had I given it any thought but Panther Key Beach was and still is a very popular spot. It is the longest and possibly the best beach in the whole Ten Thousand Islands. The fishing is excellent in the area. Shelling is fair and there are usually pieces of decorative driftwood to be found. It is an ideal spot for a picnic lunch or even camping. Consequently, many of the people who came would have come anyway to enjoy the beach. Finding a hermit in residence only made things more interesting.

Then the shack, which for years had been tightly shuttered except for occasional weekends when Dick used it, was now obviously lived in. During the day the window panels would be propped up on long poles. My little boat would be dragged up on the beach and a black dog would come frolicking out to the beach to greet anyone. People were understandably curious about what I was doing there.

I have had a few visitors while living in my tent on Brush Key, fishermen or boater whose curiosity outweighed any reluctance they might have had to encroach on my privacy. Even back then, I had enjoyed having folks stop by because it gave me a chance to show off my trails and my snug little camp. Now on Panther I got a kick out of inviting people in to see my shack and to show them my fabulous self-flushing outhouse.

I mentioned that Foster was a very popular hermit and during the few months I stayed with him I met several of his friends. Some of them started to drop by to see me on Panther. Many of the people who visited me came back a second time bringing relatives or friends. Some dropped in to see me every time they were fishing in the vicinity. Needless to say I ended up with a whole crop of new friends.

Hermits: Al Seely (Panther Key), Foster Atkinson (Dismal Key), Joe Dickman (Kice Island)

One of the most curious things about all this was the fact that most of these people … even strangers … invariably brought me things: fresh fruit, cookies, a dozen eggs, jars of jelly, books and magazines, bones and meat scraps for Willie and all kinds of good things. I have never fully understood this. Foster had the same experience but in his case it made some sense. He was, after all, a frail-looking, skinny, little man who had known many hungry years. People may have felt that he needed whatever extra food he could come by. One look at my corpulence would be enough to dispel any ideas of my being underfed. My clothes were never freshly cleaned and pressed but neither were they ragged and threadbare. What, then, prompted all the goodies? I can only surmise that it was some kind of complex psychological thing in which they wished that they could shuck off the evils of civilization and live like I do. Since they couldn't do that, the nearest thing to it was a vicarious sharing of my experience by contributing something good to it. Hell. I don't know. Maybe, I'm way out. All I am sure of is that I never refused a gift and was most happy to get them all.

Back a bit I mentioned Foster giving me a crash course in Panther Key history. This he did while strolling around the island with me, pointing out spots of interest. He went beyond this by giving me a couple of books that had sections devoted to the island and its inhabitants. Then, there was a couple of old mullet fishermen who added their versions. From these and other sources I have compiled the following short history of this most fascinating island.

The first residents of Panther Key were the Calusa Indians, the same kind of Indians who built the huge mound on Dismal Key. Some sources claim that there were Indians in Florida as far back as ten thousand years ago. This may be so, but as far as Panther Key is concerned we'll call it two thousand, give or take a few hundred years. This estimate is based on the age of the potsherds and shell tools found there. A hermit called Roy lived there for a while and he sent sample sherds to some university for carbon dating and it was determined that they were approximately two thousand years old.

Roy Ozmer hermit of Pelican Key & Foster Atkinson hermit of Dismal Key, 1965

(Photo courtesy of Everglades City High School students)

65

One source states that there was once a large shell mound on Panther Key. It is no longer there and the only evidence that it ever was there are the few scattered potsherds to be found in the mud flats that became exposed at the tip of the island during low spring tides. The reason for its disappearance is that the waves and tides and currents have been and still are washing away the front of the island and dumping it all toward the back at the rate of several feet per year.

From the air I imagine that the front or point of Panther Key would resemble a huge thumb sticking out into the Gulf of Mexico. The mud flats I have just referred to extend a couple of hundred yards beyond this point. Out there you can find stumps and roots of sizeable trees indicating that at one time the island actually extended that much further out. One of the mullet fishermen who lived his entire life on Chokoloskee told me that he remembered it like that when he was a boy. Even during the few years that I lived there I saw the bank at the point cut back some six to eight feet. The beach by my shack extended further into the bay each year by a proportionate amount.

Keeping this phenomenon in mind it is possible to imagine that centuries ago a sizeable shell mound did exist where there is nothing now but flats, which are submerged at high tide. However, it is a very curious thing that a shell mound should have been erected there in the first place. Most of the other existing mounds in this area are on islands located back in protected waters some distance from the sea, attesting to the fact that these Indians knew all about tropical storms and hurricanes. To build a mound at the very tip of Panther Key would seem to be almost suicidal.

Unfortunately, the Calusa did not leave any history in the form of Rosetta stones or Dead Sea scrolls, or hieroglyphics like the Egyptians used. All they left to posterity were their broken pots, worn tools, animal and fish bones and a few wooden artifacts. Whatever is known or guessed about these Indians, then, must be based on an interpretation of what these remains signify. Over the years I have had quite a few self styled experts in Calusa lore tell me as gospel truth what certain shell tools were used for. Some said they were used to dig with. Others said that they were for pounding. Still others said that they were fleshing tools to scrape animal hides clean. I mention this only by way of saying humbly that I have concluded by now that some of my own theories may be just as valid. And I have one about why there was a mound on Panther Key.

It is my opinion that this was not a permanent dwelling site as is the Dismal Key mound, but was used only during safe seasons of the year for the purpose of gathering fish and shellfish. I base this on the type of potsherds I found there on the flats. They were invariably much larger than any shards found on the inland mounds, some being the size of the palm of my hand. They were much thicker and coarser and utterly devoid of ornamentation. Many of the potsherds found on Dismal Key for instance, have a variety of fairly intricate and sophisticated designs worked into them. It would seem to me that the Panther Key pots were strictly utilitarian as opposed to the fancier and smaller ceremonial pots they used in their permanent locations.

Once, after a storm had scoured the mound site I found a group of potsherds all together, sticking up endwise in the mud. I was immediately excited thinking that I might have found the remains of a whole pot. I carefully removed each piece and then probed and dug gingerly until I was certain I had them all. I filled my hat and my pockets with them and took them back to the shack to was and examine. My excitement increased when they began to fit together like a jigsaw puzzle. But as soon as I got enough of the rim pieces fitted so that the curvature was established I knew I had nowhere near enough fragments to rebuild the entire pot. Actually I ended up with something like a third of one. It was enough however, to make it possible to judge the size and shape. Had I been able to reconstruct the whole pot it would have been about a foot and a half in diameter and about eight inches deep.

I was mighty proud of that find. In fact, it may have been of considerable historical value. Probably was, because an amateur anthropologist who had just returned from Yucatan and was following the theory that the Calusa had migrated from there to Florida offered me ten dollars for it. He said he wanted to donate it to the Smithsonian Institute, which he may have done. Anyway like a dope I sold it to him. I rationalized that I could probably find another one like it. Of course, I never have.

Maybe I was a dope on another score too. I said that a lot of people visited Panther Key to roam the beach hunting shells and driftwood. After my arrival I called their attention to the potsherds they could find once they knew what to look for. In the years since, the beach and the flats have been picked clean. The last time I visited there I wasn't able to find a solitary piece.

The experts tell us that the Calusa Indians had all disappeared from Florida by the year 1800. They theorize that many died off from diseases introduced by the Spanish explorers, some were taken prisoner by them, some became slaves of the northern Indians who were moving into Florida, and some perchance escaped to Cuba. No one knows of course when the last Calusa left Panther Key.

Juan Gomez

No one knows either … or at least there is no agreement … as to when Juan Gomez became a resident of Panther Key. Apparently it was sometime between 1855 and 1880. There is no helluva lot of agreement about other things in the life of this colorful pirate, for pirate he was. All sources agree that he was at one time associated with the famous Gasparilla.

First the indisputable facts about Gomez, and then the maybes. He did live on Panther Key without any doubt. Official charts label the point of Panther Key "Gomez Point." Also, he and his wife were photographed by one Kenneth Ransome of Michigan who stopped at Panther Key for fresh water while sailing from the Gulf Coast around to the Atlantic coast. I have seen several different reproductions of this famous photo and in the sharpest one, the contours of White Horse Key which is the next island north of Panther are plainly recognizable proving that the picture was in fact taken on Panther Key and nowhere else. One writer telling about this photo incident made quite a bit of the fact that an honest-to-god pirate had lived on into our modern age long enough to be photographed. But the thing that impresses me more is that this remarkably clear photo was taken as far back as 1898. Another fact that is documented is that Gomez served as a scout during the Seminole War under the command of General Zachary Taylor. Perhaps it was this service that gained him amnesty for his crimes of piracy. The last fact of which there is no doubt is that Gomez died in July 1900. Everything else about him is conjectural.

**Juan Gomez
Panther Key**

Gomez and his wife at home on Panther Key

How he died or where he may be buried is unknown. It is generally accepted that he was found drowned and tangled in fishing net. It is conjectured that he might have fallen out of his boat by accident. Another guess is that he deliberately wrapped himself in the heavily weighted net and jumped; or thirdly, that he was the victim of foul play. Which seems to cover it pretty well. If it wasn't accident, suicide, or murder, what the hell else could it have been?

It is pretty well agreed that he could not have expected to live a whole lot longer, being either 120 or 122 years of age by his own reckoning. He was either born on the Portuguese Island of Madeira in 1778 or in Madrid Spain in 1776, a date which does not tally with either of his conjectured ages at death. He is also purported to have served with Napoleon Bonaparte. In later life he is supposed to have sold bogus treasure maps, which might if true cast some doubt on the veracity of his other claims.

It is said that Gomez tried to raise goats and that panthers ate them all, thereby giving the island its name. This legend may very well have been true, because many years later the hermit, called Roy, living on the same island, found his dog with a broken back and disemboweled. It was obviously the work of a panther, verifying that Panther Key was aptly named.

The biggest mystery is whether or not Gomez took a share of Gasparilla's looted pirate treasure with him when he escaped, and if so what did he do with it?

There are some of the local mullet fishermen and guides who swear by all that's holy to them that he did have a treasure of gold coins buried beneath his thatched roof shack and that it was dug-up years ago. By whom, they never say. I fancy they are the only ones who believe this story because during Roy's[3] years on Panther the treasure hunters, as he put it, "Still hopefully come … and disconsolately go." During my five years there they still come to search and left empty handed.

One day, to give an example of my experiences with treasure hunters, a young man and his wife came ashore. He had a metal detector in one hand and was happily flipping a Spanish gold coin in the other which he proudly showed me to be one of the famous pieces of eight.

"I hear there's some pirate treasure buried on your island," he said introducing himself.

"I very much doubt it. " I said, "Not that I want to dash cold water on your hopes right off like that, but people have been hunting it for years and years and no one's ever come up with anything but old beer cans and rusty nails."

"Good," he enthused, "then its still here. Where's a good spot to start looking?"

"Sorry to have to disappoint you some more," I said, "but the pirate's old home site is under water right now and will be until late this afternoon when the tide goes out."

"Fine," he said, "I'll be back then."

At five o'clock or so the couple came back only this time he was holding a can of beer in one hand and flipping his coin in the other.

---

[3] Hermit Roy Ozmer

"Guess'll have t'wait till next week," he told me in a slurring voice. "We had a few beers too many and dropped the metal detector overboard. I got it back, but it don't work so well now."

The following week he was back with his wife and another young fellow.

"Got me a new detector," he informed me right off, "a real fine one this time. How's the tide today ... low enough?" I said that it was and we walked on down to the point. Our progress was slow due to his scanning the whole beach with his "squealer" as we went. I showed them the approximate location of 'Gomez' shack (determined by the remains of an old wood cask partially buried in the sand) and wished them luck. I had taken my spinning rod along and while they wandered around on the mud flats I fished.

After and hour or so they came back to where I was casting and putting the detector down on the beach told me they had had no luck.

"Maybe your gizmo isn't working too well," I suggested, "I've seen quite a few of them and have yet to see one which really works."

"Oh, this one's a dandy," they assured me gesturing toward the detector on the beach, "...cost $149."

Hardly were the words out of his mouth when his dandy detector which had been lying mute on the beach for five minutes; suddenly began to emit the wailing squeals expected of it when it is poised over something metallic.

"That sure is a dandy," I said.

Almost as big a mystery, to me at any rate, is the matter of fresh water on Panther Key. Historically, this island was a regular fresh water stop for sailing vessel plying the Gulf Coast of Florida. But, I'll be damned if I could find any. There are a number of sloughs (called "slews" locally) in the interior of the island. I have sampled them all and found the water salty. I also dug a dozen or more test holes and invariably found the same thing. The only guess I can come up with is that the source of fresh water must have been located out on the point somewhere and since been washed away by the erosion I described earlier. One bit of evidence for this is the fact that I did find some pieces of sandstone out in that area. Possibly at one time there was an underlying bed of sandstone sufficiently large to trap and hold rainwater. But this is simply a guess.

Also washed away now are the remains of what was probably Juan Gomez' own private water cask. During my years there it was part of my conducted tours to show visitors the eroding wooden staves which protruded some six or eight inches above the sand in a spot not far from the site of his home as near as I could place it.

When I moved away I took a short piece as a souvenir, thinking to paint something on it, but damned if somebody didn't steal it once when I was away. So all that remains of Juan Gomez is the sketchy but colorful story of his long life.

There is no hard information about anyone actually living on Panther Key between 1900 when Gomez died and 1961 when Roy[4] had his hermit shack on

---

[4] Hermits of Ten Thousand Islands include: Juan Gomez of Panther Key, Arthur Leslie Darwin of Possum Key, Roy Ozmer of Pelican Key, Leon Whilden of Everglades, Al Seely of Dismal Key, Eardley Foster

Pelican Key destroyed by hurricane Donna and was forced to move out of the National Park boundaries. He built his next home on the southeast side of Gomez point … the opposite shore from mine.

Al Seely examining the remains of Juan Gomez's water barrel)
(Photo courtesy of Everglades City High School students)

I recall that the day I had the interview with Mrs. Morton at the University of Miami she dug out a two-page newspaper story to show me. There was a picture of a lean bearded man with a beret sitting on a lump of wormrock in front of a crude shack. The story caption was "Hermit of Panther Key." She told me it would be much to my advantage to look this fellow up after I got out here. She was certain he would have much to teach me about surviving in the islands. As luck would have it, he was forced by failing eyesight and ill health to leave this area before I got here so I never had the privilege of meeting him. I have met dozens of people who knew him well and who have told me so much about him that I almost feel as if I knew him anyway. From the many anecdotes and comments about him I can only conclude that he was very popular and a larger-than-life character.

Nothing much remains of his home site on Panther but some rotting boards, the bent aluminum frame of a lawn chair and a pile of liquor bottles. Apparently heavy drinking and hermiting go together somehow.

Atkinson of Dismal Key, Henry Dalmas of an unnamed island, and one woman, Martha Frock, of Everglades. Resource pamphlet: Prop Roots, Vol. II Hermits from The Mangrove Country of The Everglades, published by Collier County Public Schools, 1980.

Like me, he had cut a few trails across the island, but unlike me, he was ambitious enough to build a rustic bridge where one of his trails crossed a slough. Another of his enterprises, which can still be seen, is a tree house he built as an emergency hurricane shelter. I shouldn't care to trust my life to it after all these years but there is no doubt that it was sturdy enough in his time, being fastened to the huge Sea grape trunk by steel cables.

Houseboat gang of 1967
Back row: Joe Dickman, Totch Brown and wife(?), & unknown lady.
Front row: Dottie Barlow (later Pettit), Charlie (last name unknown
but tended bar at the Ideal Fish Camp, Pettit's place on Caxambas and
was Joe Dickman's roommate when they lived in the old Barfield
house), Lawrence Pettit, and Nelson Barlow.
(Photo courtesy of Bob Steele))

According to the legends about him that have come down to me, he eventually left the shack to live in a huge houseboat. One of the type known as a "lighter" down here, big as a regular house. With manpower and boat power this was dragged ashore on a tiny island in the bay midway between Panther Key and Hog Key. Here he made a serious error, though he didn't live there long enough to see the results of it.

Houseboat at Dismal Key
(Photo courtesy of Bob Steele)

His move from his shack to the houseboat was prompted by the proliferation of mosquitoes. Not being satisfied with the breezes on the small island to keep the bugs down, he proceeded to cut many of the larger mangrove trees. With the roots rotting away and no longer able to hold the soil, the island has continually washed away till it is practically non-existent. Three years ago the houseboat broke up in a tropical depression and is long gone too. Roy, back in civilization, which, proved too much for him, took his own life.

Al Seely and his dog 1969
(Courtesy of Bob Steele)

Chapter 8

Shelling and Mini-stories

So now we're back to the second hermit of Panther Key … me … and the five years I lived there.

Shack on Panther Key, Al Seely's home for five years.
(Photo courtesy of Everglades City High School students)

First a philosophical observation. It is interesting I think to speculate on how really unimportant some of us are in the overall scheme of things. Over a period of more than two thousand years the various residents of Panther Key have come and gone… those we know about and possibly some we don't, and there is practically nothing left to show that any of us were ever there.

I was just about to become more ironical still by pointing out that at least from the standpoint of durability, the fragments of pottery made by the most primitive and uncivilized of the Panther Key people have lasted longest of all. But this may not be true. Who knows how long Roy's collection of booze bottles will take to disintegrate?

The old pirate's water cask lasted for nearly one hundred years, but now that is gone it would be very difficult to find any other evidences of his life there except for a rare piece of rusted iron or broken china.

I kept busy as hell for my five years and there is nothing to show that I ever lived there except one tree which I transplanted from another island and which may survive until the next hurricane.

Yeah, I was busy enough. Much of it was routine busy-ness. Since I started living there at the beginning of the cold weather I had to get a supply of wood together which entailed finding the dead trees which, being already seasoned, would burn readily, then cutting them down, clearing a path to drag them back to the shack and building a saw horse to cut them into stove lengths.

I cleared out Roy's old trails and cut a few new ones for the benefit of my visitors who like to take a tour around the island.

I fished some most every day and walked the long beach once or twice daily for the benefit of Ole Willie who wasn't much for going off on his own.

I don't know just how it came about, but as the months passed I found myself eating fewer native foods, except for fish, and more store-bought ones. Charlotte's supply trips brought an ever-increasing amount and variety of things to eat which being mostly canned goods necessitated a place to get rid of the empty cans. This resulted in my digging a huge pit at a discreet distance from the shack. When it filled I had to dig another one and so on.

Oh, Hey! Maybe some of those cans will be around a few hundred years from now to show that I once lived there. If anyone should happen to dig them up, that is. What a lovely legacy!

The next order of business was to see if I could do a bit of business collecting shells and other marine specimens to sell to a wholesale house in Goodland. I felt it was time I made a buck or two. My long-range money goal was to get a larger boat and motor, my short range to be able to slake a thirst that was sneaking up on me.

Starfish were plentiful out on the flats and were the most lucrative, bringing around five cents apiece in those days. But don't think it was simply a matter of picking them up and lugging them off to market.

When I was a kid my parents made and annual trip to the beach and finding a starfish was to me then what finding a pearl would be today. Except that by the time I got it home it was shriveled all out of shape and more than slightly aromatic. Since this may be the experience of others, I'll give you a quick run through on the way I prepared the starfish to stay in shape indefinitely.

First I'd prepare my cooking mixture of half a gallon of formaldehyde and half a gallon of water. I should say curing rather than cooking though that's the term Foster used. I then put two or three inches of seawater in the flat bottom of my Jon boat. A shallow tide pool would have worked well. Then spread two or three-dozen starfish around in the water not touching each other. In a few minutes they would begin to uncurl and spread into their distinctive star shape. As each was posing its prettiest, I'd scoop it out of the boat and drop it in the formaldehyde, which killed it instantly and locked in position. A few hours in the solution would be sufficient to preserve them indefinitely.

Formaldehyde is rough stuff to work with. It stinks like hell, irritates the nasal passages, and burns the skin. It must be used with caution. To get the stars out of the solution and onto the drying board painlessly, I used a pair of cooking tongs. Rubber gloves would do the job all right, I reckon. Two or three days in the sun, turning them over once or twice was sufficient to dry them and clear away the fumes. All that was left was to count and box them.

The next best selling item was the whelk shells. Mainly because these are fairly large and since they are sold by the bushel, it didn't take many to fill a basket. Some of the real huge ones – giant whelks – I sold individually. Whelks had to be cleaned too, but this was a simple matter of dumping them in boiling water for ten minutes and then picking the animal out with an ice pick.

That all sounds humdrum but it wasn't really because when you collect specimens in quantity you find freaks. I had at one time quite a collection of starfish with extra arms or double arms or jointed arms or arms coming out of arms. I had right and left-handed whelks and albinos and a whole spectrum of beautifully colored shells. I say I had them at one time. No more. Like the idiot I am, I gave them all away.

The shelling and star fishing business did eventually make a small contribution to getting a better boat, and also provided a pretty fair binge every few months.

Well, hell, better than every few days like before.

But, after a couple of years I gave it up.

The shelling, that is.

Naturally.

First, I had about picked the island clean and also I found an easier way to make a buck. More on that later.

You might think that by walking the same beach nearly every day for five years that I would have eventually seen everything there was to see and learned all there was to know about it. This was not so, of course. Every so often I'd encounter some new, strange and wondrous thing. The same is true of Dismal Key where I now live and I venture to say that if I am so fortunate as to spend the rest of my life out here, I will never run out of new things to discover and marvel at.

Some of these new things were mysteries to me and have remained mysteries. Other mysteries eventually got solved, not that I ever tried very hard to solve them. Usually some one would come along who knew more than I about them, or I'd stumble onto the pertinent information in books or nature magazines. At any rate I'll share a random sampling of these happenings just to give you a fuller flavor of life on a Gulf Coast island.

The singing fish

One evening just after dark my dogs…

Oops. Sorry.

Gotta sidetrack here a step to explain dogs, plural.

Yup. I got "Barbie" just about the time the singing fish come for a visit. I don't need to go into a whole production about it, but Charlotte was in those days a one-woman S.P.C.A. Naturally this resulted in her having an ever increasing dog population in her suburban home. At one point she rescued two or one gave birth to two or some damn thing. Anyway she had two dogs that fought forever and incessantly. To relieve that situation I agreed to take one of them … a black female terrier of some bristle-nosed, curly-tailed, mixed breed. I wasn't too happy about it because she was not friendly with people as Willie was. Not mean exactly, just standoffish and "don't get too near to me when I growl." She later became my favorite and broke my heart when she died of heartworm. To get back …

One evening just after dark my dogs began a ruckus out on the beach and, of course, I had to go out to see what was up. When I got there, they were standing at the edge of the water barking at something just off shore. At first all I could detect was a sort of boiling in the water such as you see sometimes when a school of minnows is passing by. But between barks I could hear something too. As near as I can describe it, it was a sound similar to that which might be made by a group of children gargling at a pitch somewhere around "A" above middle "C", except not as loud. I kept shining my spotlight into the water, but unfortunately it was on the muddy side that night so that all I could be sure of was that it was seething with fish of some sort and in breaking the surface amide thousands of bubbles, they were making this weird singing sound.

I immediately thought of mullet because mullet are extraordinarily wacky fish anyway. They will leap in the air and belly flop back into the water, or stand on their tails and gyrate like a dervish, or moil around each other like slimy wrestlers. They aren't always this way, of course. They seem to go on some kind of fishy binge now and again. When they are on a kick like that, though you have only to hold a bright light in your boat and they'll obligingly jump right in. They'll jump right out again, too.

We seem to be getting into double mystery here, the strange behavior of mullet and the identity of the singing fish if they were not mullet. Anyway, the first time one of the old native mullet fishermen came along I hailed him, thinking if anyone should be familiar with such a phenomenon it would be a man who had spent most of his life tracking and catching fish. But when I described the concert, he shook his head in puzzlement. He had never heard mullet make any such sounds, nor any other fish. Was I sober?

Aha! That's just it.

I was.

I have asked at least twenty people since who might know, but the singing fish remain a mystery.

The sand writers

One day I began to notice what I eventually called sand writing or sand drawing or beach hieroglyphics. On a receding tide where the beach sand would be wave lapped smooth there would appear welts about a half inch high extending in zig zaggy patterns for several feet. From their appearance I judged that some tiny creature was humping along just under the wet surface of the sand mounding it as it moved along. More than once, many times actually, I've taken a twig and with all the skill at my command have poked gently along the entire trail, carefully dislodging the roof in the hope of catching the architect. And I never have. I asked Foster about it once and he said he'd had the same experience ...never caught the culprit.

But you see the intriguing thing here is that we both assumed from the appearance of these welts they were made by a bug, or tiny snail, or crab, or something made them. But since we never found one ... who knows? It could be something else entirely. At least as far as I *know* it could be.

The ass-backward eel

This next weird creature is no mystery now. It was for a while until I identified it in a dictionary of fishes, but it is so amazing that it is worth telling about. The first time I saw one lying on the beach I was certain it had to be a snake. It was tiny, maybe ten inches long and about as big around as my little finger brown with whitish spots. I poked at it with my walking stick thinking it was dead and the outgoing tide had left the carcass stranded there. It was anything but. It attacked the stick with remarkable vigor, and I was glad it was the stick getting the licks and not my toes. After poking it a bit I got it into a jar and pickled it in formaldehyde for the amazement of my visitors.

One day a young couple were doing the beach hoping to find some shells, I told them to watch for little trails in the sand ... not humped up trails as I've just described for the mysterious sand writers, but hollowed out as if someone had dragged a stick along. Then at the end of such a trail, I told them to poke a finger down into the wet sand and wriggle it around. If they didn't hit anything to try the other end of the trail. At one end or the other you can usually turn up a live shark's eye, baby's ear, cerith, or augur or something.

I wandered off, then, leaving them to their poking when all of a sudden the girl let out a bloodcurdling screech. Her husband and I rushed over and there she stood speechless pointing to one of these squirming snake-like things.

"Did it bite you?" I asked first off, thinking of those teeth.

"My God ... what is it?" she gasped.

"It didn't bite you then?"

"You mean it bites?" she asked.

"Very likely, " I replied. "How did you find it?"

She pointed to the burrow in the sand. You could see where she had riffled it with her finger.

"Boy, you were lucky" I said, "poking him out of the sand like that."

"You should have told me," she accused.

"But, I didn't know they made burrows like that."

"Well, now you know."

"Yeah," I agreed.

All this time the eel was squirming around angrily, but then suddenly, right before our eyes, it began to squirm backwards, inserting its tail in the sand and before it hardly had time to register on our astonished eyes, it had burrowed itself completely out of sight.

"That slimy bastard," I told them, "is called the 'sharp-tailed eel.' Now I know why."

I have watched them several times since then, and it is truly uncanny the way they can disappear ass-backwards with such speeds.

The inside-outers

If you were living alone on an island and you went out one morning to find the beach littered with hundreds of blobs of greenish-gray protoplasm stuff, blobs which you could see on close inspection to be alive and pulsating and creatures, moreover which were not there the night before, what would be the first thing you might think of? Invasion from outer space, right? Well, maybe you wouldn't. Maybe you have not gone through a science fiction phase as I have in my younger years. Anyway, that is what entered my mind when I encountered just such a sight one sunny morning toward spring of my first year on Panther Key. I'll admit that because of it I had a moment or two of uneasiness until my better judgment came to the rescue.

These blobs were about the size of a baseball if you can visualize a very limp baseball, having no particular shape. Maybe like dollops of soft, moldy bread dough. The color pattern was variegated green and reddish green on a brownish-gray ground. As I say, they were alive, though not moving except for a slow inner pulsating. I prodded one gently with my stick and two things happened. It folded in on itself, sort of scrooched up into a smaller blob and at the time exuded a puddle of beautiful red-purple dye. The tide was going out as I recall and as the small waves washed the beach, one after another of these horrid looking globs would be washed ashore. I looked out into the water then to see where they were coming from and saw one or two swimming. Those were so different from the ones curled or folded on the beach that at first I couldn't believe they were the same critter. When swimming they were about a foot long, cigar shaped with rubbery wings on each side which undulate slowly.

I don't need to say that I asked an old timer about these pukey things at the first opportunity.

"Oh, them things," he said. "Them are ink fish. Red ink. Always in the red ... get it? Hoo haw-haw."

"Are they poisonous or anything?" I asked.

"Nah ... just not worth a shit for nothing"

"Not edible I suppose?"

"Edible? ...Oh, you mean eat ... Jesus, who'd want to eat blobs of shit like that?"

I refrained from telling him that squid is a delicacy in some parts of the world and these ink fish looked no more repulsive to me than squid.

So the creatures like from outer space were identified for me as ink fish in 1968. In 1976 a friend of mine sent me a nature studies leaflet about this same creature under the common name of "Sea Hare."

It turns out that whether known as Ink Fish or Sea Hare, the thing is actually an *Aplysia Dactylomela* (whatever the hell that means) and is a type of snail. But this is an inside out snail. Whereas the snails we are mostly familiar with live inside a shell, this *Aplysia* character has its shell tucked away inside the body.

The muddy murex

Another of the little mysteries, which I will inject here, may not be a mystery to anyone but me. It involves an aspect of nature, which could be a whole area for study in itself; namely, the uses of color. Some of these uses are familiar to me such as the color of flowers to attract bees and butterflies, or the imitative colors of some things to repel attack, or the color differences in the sexes. From these and other instances I have always considered that color in nature is never a random thing, so I am at a loss to understand the use of, or need for, the delicate coloring of the murex shell. Because, you see, all the murex shells I have ever found were completely covered with mud. Only after cleaning with Clorox and dipping them in muriatic acid do the colors emerge. What's the purpose, then, of the colors?

It's possible, I suppose, that they travel greater distances than I think, maybe moving into these muddy bays from out in the deep water where their colors would not be fouled. Or there may be some other explanation. All I know is that when I have discussed it with other people we always seem to end up with some esoteric, philosophical ideas that throw no light on the problem. It is still a mystery to me anyway.

Lo the Crows!

I'd be the first to agree that girl watching is more fun than bird watching but even in this age of sexual revolution the hermit life has some limitations. So I am a bird watcher. Not a dedicated one by any means. I don't even have binoculars nor do I ever go to any trouble to see them. If the birds are there and they are doing something unusual, I watch them.

This all started with crows and I got involved with crows because I spoil my dogs. It ties up this way. In addition to the best of commercial dog food, their dish usually contained liberal scraps of corned beef or other canned meat or fish from my own meals. Like all spoiled children they have become picky eaters with the result that often I had half a dish of dog food to throw away. Throwing away consisted of stepping out onto my porch and flinging the stuff into the bushes.

One day, the squawking of many crows finally got on my nerves and thus called my attention to them. I discovered they were having a friendly scrap over the dog food I had pitched out. I got such a bang out of watching them cram their beaks so full it kept dribbling out, then trying to steal from each other that I began keeping them supplied with food. I also put out a pan of water for them on a little fold up TV table.

I'm sure they realized that I meant them no harm. They must even have realized that I was the provider of their daily goodies. The reason I knew this is that on the rare days I forgot to toss out something for them, they reminded me of my thoughtlessness by setting up a terrific din just outside my door.

One of the first bits of crow intelligence I observed was their system of guarding each other at feeding time. First they'd fly into the nearby trees, talking thirteen to the dozen, waiting for me to heave out the daily ration. Then two or three would fly down into the low bushes beside the cleared space where the food and water dish were. There, they'd teeter around, peering this way and that out of first one eye and then the other until they were convinced the coast was clear. One would then hop to the ground and pick up as many morsels as he could possible cram into his beak. Should anything threaten, the guards still in the bush would sound the alarm and the feeding bird took to the hills. If nothing happened, the one feeding flew off with his beak load and after further reconnoitering a second bird would drop to the ground while another came to stand guard. There were usually five crows that came around regularly and more than once I've watched the complete rotation of guarding and feeding, the first feeder coming back to get in line again for a second go round at the food. But, I was never able to watch where they took the stuff. They must have a hidey-hole for it somewhere nearby, which they probably loaded up while the grub was handy. They undoubtedly ate it later and at their leisure. Being intrigued by their greedy habit of stuffing their beaks, I once tossed out some whole slices of stale bread. You guessed it. Of they flew, each carrying a complete slice. The dog food I use comes in hard little chunks about the size of the tip of your thumb. Sometimes, if the crows felt secure and after they had carried off a few loads, they'd stay around and gobble up some of the smaller pieces. The larger pieces were apparently too big to swallow whole, but it didn't take them long to figure out how to dunk them in the water dish to soften them up.

Another example of crow intelligence is illustrated in the following incident … that is, if I have analyzed their behavior correctly. Walking the beach one day I found a dead black skimmer. If you are not familiar with this bird let me tell you that it is a very beautiful bird indeed with its grey-black, graceful wings and long red beak. I picked the bird up and examined it but could find no clues as to what had caused its death. I was about to pitch it into the ocean when it occurred to me that I might figure out something decorative to do with the feathers, which were clean and shiny. I took it home, carrying it by the legs, which caused the limp wings to flop around in a grotesque manner.

It was getting on toward lunchtime when I got back to the shack and my crows were gathered in their usual tree waiting for the daily handout. Suddenly, they exploded into the God-awfullest din of caws and shrieks I'd ever heard from them. They took to the skies, made one whirl over the shack and were long gone.

I can only guess that when they saw me coming along with what may have looked to them like a captive bird in my hand, one moreover, being carried in an extremely undignified manner, their opinion of me underwent a drastic change. From a benefactor I had become a killer and a menace. As I say this opinion is only guesswork. But the crows stayed away for nearly a week before deciding it was safe to resume their daily feedings.

The rest of this discussion of crows includes both the Panther Key crows and the five or six I still have on Dismal Key.

Most fun of all, is watching the crows in the spring and summer when they bring along their brood of fledglings. These offspring are so nearly full grown that would not have noticed them had their voices been mature. But like teenage boys their cries start off in a full bass "caw" cry, then crack and end up in a treble squeak. They can fly all right, but are not too hot at landing on the small branches where they usually perch. They flutter-flop onto the branch, grabbing it frantically with their claws, and while teetering back and forth, give out cries of fright that sound like "Oh – Oh – Oh." Sometimes they lose their balance altogether and fall into the air with a last treble shriek, suddenly remembering how to fly and so trying again. While the youngsters are around I have noticed that the adult crows are real sticklers for the guard and cover routine, doing a lot of yawping in the process. teaching by example, no doubt, also by lecture

For a while I thought I might catch on to their code language because I noticed that their calls came in certain groupings. For instance, if one crow calls, "caw – caw," another answers "caw – caw." If it is "caw-caw-caw," the reply is the same. I even got so far as to imitate the cries and get replies from them in the same sequence. But who the hell know what they are trying to say. The only crow communication that not only I, but even the dogs, understand is when the crows see something moving in the woods ... a coon or bobcat or something. Then they'll set up a regular frantic din of warning.

I used to think that "caw" was the extent of a crow's vocabulary but it is far from being so. Sometimes they croon a sort of low, mellifluous "ma-ma: ma-ma." At other times they make sounds like German gutturals, like a dry gargle. Still again they emit soft fluting whistles. I don't know how many times I have heard what seemed to be a new and different call and went to check it out, only to find a big old crow perched in a tree blinking wisely at me.

Mama plover's tragedy

This little lady pulled the broken wing act on me one morning as I was going from my shack to the beach. I knew nothing about the nesting habits of plovers but it was obvious that she had a nest nearby so I proceeded to hunt around. I found it, sure enough, right in plain sight and spang in the middle of my path. It was just a little scooped out hole in the sand with four speckled eggs in it. I looked at the eggs and I looked at the plover and I'm damned if I know yet how such big eggs could have come out of such a tiny bird. But, I reckon they did.

She was flitting nervously back and forth and about to have a hissy so they must have been her eggs. I told her she was pretty stupid to go putting her nest practically under foot, I decided to give her a helping hand. I cut a couple dozen short branches and stuck them up right in the sand in a protective ring around her nest, figuring the leaves would provide a bit of shade for her during the hatching period. When it was finished I backed off a fair distance and watched till she investigated this new thing, passed judgment on it and settled back on her nest. A couple of hours later I had occasion to be out there again and here is mama plover still flapping around and cheeping up a storm. Ole Willie, figuring I'd made a patch of shade for his special benefit was curled up, dozing peacefully inside the ring of branches. I gentled him and for a wonder, only one of the eggs was cracked. I was sorry about that, but better three than none. I replaced the branches with a ring of straight sticks, with no leaves. That would keep anyone or anything from stepping on them anyway. But next morning when I went out to check the remaining eggs were smashed and the bereaved plover was gone. Having gotten involved in the affair as I did, I couldn't help feeling a bit forlorn myself; to say nothing of being very curious about what happened to her eggs. Some predatory bird, a coon, or snake? Don't know.

Chapter 9

Hermit's Folly

It took three shots to get the right boat for my needs. The ten-foot Jon boat I came out with was too little. With my two-hundred pounds and Willie's forty or so in it, the craft had barely eight inches of freeboard which is definitely not enough in any sea with more than a light to moderate chop. Furthermore it was unstable. Going along with Willie in the front, every time he shifted from sided to side, I had to counter shift on the rear seat to keep it level. This gets hard on one's ass after awhile.

The second boat was too big. Not that it was any forty-foot, flying bridge, cabin cruiser or anything like that. It was only a second hand twenty-foot wooden lap strake open boat powered by a fifty-horse power motor. But it was still too much boat for one ole hermit to cope with, as you shall see. I called it the "Hermit's Folly." I think I suspected from the very beginning that I might have some problems with it though I didn't know just what kind.

The third one, like baby bear's bed in the nursery story was just right. It is (I still have it) a fourteen-foot aluminum boat with adequate freeboard and very stable … yet one that can be rowed if the 9.9 horse motor quits and that can be handled readily enough on shore.

Back to the Folly…

The first trouble I had with that boat came on its first run, but in that instance the folly was with the hermit, not the boat.

We had purchased the boat in Ft. Lauderdale during a Christmas visit to Charlotte. When she brought me back I put the boat in the water at Goodland, gassed it up and loaded in the supplies. The bit motor kicked right off and settled down to a powerful purr. I kissed Charlotte goodbye. Willie and I settled ourselves comfortably on the cushioned front seat and feeling more like a prosperous sportsman than a hermit, I took the wheel of this trim looking craft and headed out into the channel.

Up to this point the only experience I had ever had with boats was with the little dinghy I came out with, so I had no basis for comparing performance. Nevertheless after a couple of miles I had the feeling that this new boat was unusually sluggish. A couple of miles more and I found out I was right – and why. My feet were getting wet. There was at least six inches of water in the bottom.

This wasn't particularly alarming to me because I had read somewhere that wooden boats have a tendency to leak when first out into the water until the boards swell. I moved as many of my supply sacks out of the water as possible and went on.

Once home on Panther Key I ran her right onto the sand beach, tied her off, bailed her out, and salvaged what I could of the water-soaked supplies. I recall that a five-pound sack of corn meal was ruined.

The next morning I found the boat about half full of water. So full actually that it was not floating. It was only a real stroke of luck that the water was shallow all along the beach. Otherwise she'd have been completely sunk. Very obviously something was wrong for it to be leaking that badly. So as soon as I could get her bailed out again … which was no mean task … I took her back into Goodland to a Marina there to see what could be done about it.

"Is there anyone here that could check over the bottom of this boat?" I asked the first guy I saw as I pulled in the Marina dock. "Do you have a whaddya callem 'ways' or something?"

"What seems to be the trouble?" he asked.

"Well, I just bought this boat and put it in the water for the first time yesterday and it's leaking like hell." I told him pointing to the water that was again slopping over the floorboards. I added, "All this leaked in just coming up from Panther Key."

"Is your drain plug in?" he asked then.

"Drain plug! What drain plug?" I said.

"Here, let me take a look … whereupon he jumped into the boat and his arm disappeared in the bilge under the rear seat.

"Just as I thought," he told me over his shoulder, "No wonder you were leaking, your drain plug is open. I don't think you'll have any more trouble now that I've closed it."

Thus did I gain a new point in my painful education about the operation and maintenance of boats and motors.

On the way back to Panther I was so elated at finding that the Folly didn't really leak after all that I shoved the throttle open all the way. Imagine my surprise when the boat sat up on top of the water and planed. I made the twelve miles back in little over thirty minutes.

For a while I was quite thrilled with this boat. I got a bang out of having a cushioned front seat and steering wheel, just like a car. It started like a car too, by turning the ignition key. However, in those first runs to and from Goodland I discovered that it was an unbelievable gas hog. Being accustomed to automobiles that ordinarily averaged up to twenty miles to the gallon, it was a shock to find that the Folly didn't get more than two miles per gallon. It required a full six-gallon tank to make the twelve-mile run into town. Another tank to come back. Figuring a quart of oil to each tank of gas, the cost of a round trip came close to six dollars in those days. So, although it was delightful to know that I could run into town in thirty minutes as opposed to four hours in the Jon boat, I knew right away that I would not be making the trip any more often, new boat or no. Nor would I be able to run around much for fishing or exploring.

If I remember correctly, it was a couple of weeks after that first trip to Goodland before I had occasion to use the boat again when I decided to run over to Foster's and let him see the Folly. I got in, sat down at the wheel, put the key, turned it … nothing but a sickly growl. Dead battery.

Generally it's not like me to think of important things, but for some strange reason I did make sure when I bought it that the motor could be started by hand with a starter rope. I went back to give it a pull and I can assure you that hand starting a fifty-horse motor is a far cry from pulling a three and one-half horse. But it started and by the time I had returned from Dismal Key, the battery was charged. Not that it did any good because, I didn't use the boat again for a week or two by which time it had gone dead again. Well, I went through that rigamarole for a few months, getting her hand started and charging up the battery, or having it charged at the Marina when I was in town, only to have it go dead again between runs. When I got sick and tired of it, I hung the ignition key on a nail in the shack, threw the battery overboard, and thereafter started it by hand, developing some pretty good muscles into the bargain.

Next came the barnacles. I had always dragged the Jon boat up on the bank and left it high and dry when not in use which kept the barnacles from growing on it, but this monster of a Folly had to be in the water all the time. I first became aware of something wrong when it began to get sluggish again yet was not leaking. I asked someone about it and they suggested that I might have barnacles that would slow it down a lot. I checked and sure enough, there was a solid mat of the damn things all over the bottom … or as far under the bottom as I could feel with my hand in all directions. The average boat owner would simply pay to have his craft put on the ways and have the bottom scraped and painted. This particular hermit couldn't even dream about that extravagance, so … Mr. Master of Makeshift …front and center!

I have tried at least four times to describe in words the thingamajig that I built, I give up. It's clear enough to me because I built the dam thing after all, but I simply can't believe that anyone else could get the picture from my poor attempts at describing the thing. So let's say that I built a kind of wall of four or five inch logs about three feet high and solidly planted in the beach sand so that it would not wash-away.

This crazy looking rig was so located that at high tide I could pull the Folly across the logs with the bow on the beach and when the tide went out the stern would be sitting on the wall. Then, by digging a hole under the boat, I would crawl under and scrape off the barnacles. But what a job! Instead of peeling off in nice cooperative manner they'd jump and fly all over me and since the barnacles were alive, they'd squirt all over me too, as I cut them off. I ended up smelling like clam chowder. Luckily, it was a job I only had to do every four or five months.

The main reason the Folly was too much boat for one man living on an island surrounded by shallow water was its weight. With the fifty-horse motor … what? Five hundred pounds altogether maybe? Hell, I don't know. All I know is that if it went high and dry at low tide there was no way under the sun that I could move it. If it had some water under it I could sometimes lever it into deeper water with a long heavy pole heaving it along a few inches at a time. Mostly though it was a high tide boat.

Once I got the bright idea that since I had all the time in the world, if I dug steadily day after day after day I could eventually dig a deep enough channel leading back into the lagoon behind the shack so that I could get the damn boat in and out anytime. It didn't work. Oh, I dug and dug. Blisters, aching muscles, sweat. I dug. I got a fairly good stretch of the channel done too before a storm came along and the huge waves filled it with sand overnight. This took care of that bright idea.

Another trouble with a boat that size is that it is just about impossible to paddle it or pole it along if the motor breaks down. With any wind or trying to move against a fast running tide it was completely impossible. I was fortunate in that the time or two I had motor trouble someone came along and towed me in.

The Folly had its good points though. There was a canvas top and detachable side curtains so that it could be buttoned up all around in case of rain. It even had a windshield wiper. It had a six-foot beam and room enough so that I could fix a bed on the back seat, take a stove along and camp in it. Foster told me once that I could find some good shells on Cape Romano so I decided once to run over and stay for a few days and make a haul of shells. Thing started out beautifully. I arrived early in the morning, found a good anchorage, and spent a busy day gathering several bushels of shells. At sundown I cooked up a little meal on my kerosene stove, fed Willie, listened to the radio a bit and sacked out. Sometime during the night I awoke with a definite sensation of falling. As a matter of fact I did more or less fall off the seat I was sleeping on and when I stood up I still felt as if I were going to fall. The only thing that came to mind was some strange loss of equilibrium due to inner ear infection or some damn thing. I rummaged around from my spotlight and discovered the reason. Not inner ear trouble. The tide had gone out leaving the boat high and dry and tilted at about a thirty-degree angle.

In the morning the wind came up. I listened to the weather reports, which predicted high winds for that day at least. That called for a decision. I could either elect to stay put for a couple of days or more, moving to slightly deeper water to avoid the cockeyed sleeping, or I could get the hell out of there. Not having much faith that the wind would subside in a day or two, I got the hell out, and none too soon. Coming back across the open Gulf it was already so rough that waves were breaking over the bow and splashing into the boat. Willie got seasick, adding to the mess. After plowing through those waves for four or five miles, I turned tail, to get a following sea and headed for the nearest protected waters, making a long circuitous way home. When I figured it all up; the income from the shells against the expense of the trip … to say nothing of my time, I found my profit on the venture was less than two dollars. But, as I say, the Folly had its points. In a smaller boat I wouldn't have been able to get home at all.

After a couple of years the motor began to give out, which is not surprising since it was nine years old when I bought it. From then on, each trip to town was a gamble. Somehow, I always made it in and back but hardly ever without a breakdown and a lot of fooling with plugs and carburetor and messing with wires and much pulling. In the third year the remote gearshift control refused to work. I had to put it in gear manually on the motor itself, then run forward, climb over the front seat and grab the steering wheel. There was hardly one trip after that without my coming home with skinned shins. Then the remote throttle quit. Thereafter, I had to operate entirely from the stern. Next one of the cylinders quit firing. The mechanic at the Marina informed me that it would require an expensive overhaul to repair it. Since it would still run, though at a reduced speed, I decided not to spend any more money on it.

In August of 1970 my son came to visit me for a couple of weeks. When it was time to take him back to town, I got the Folly started and we began to crawl across the bay. For some reason the motor quit and when I tried to start it again the starter rope parted in the middle. I looked at the rope, looked at my son and I made a pronouncement. I said, "Well … that's the fucking end. The double fucking end. No more. Finite. Etc. The Folly has made its last run!" We poled and paddled back to shore. I hailed a passing boat to take my boy to town.

At the next unusually high tide I pulled the folly as far up on the beach as I possibly could where it steadily and consistently disintegrated. Perhaps that would have been an honorable end for the old Folly. How many dilapidated and skeleton boats, rotting peacefully on a beach have been immortalized in paintings! But she was true to her name to the ignominious end. Some friends of mine wanted to take her out and sink her to make an artificial reef to improve the fishing. Having no more use for her, I agreed. I helped them tip the huge heavy motor over the transom and into the much-warped bottom to serve as ballast. We got her afloat and they towed her away, taking an axe to chop holes in the bottom to be sure she'd sink. But when they returned they told me that as she went down she turned over, the motor fell out and went to the bottom and the hull floated away. Some weeks later a passing fisherman told me he'd found the remains washed into the mangroves a couple of miles inland … where I imagine it still is.

Al Seely and his dog

(Photo courtesy of Mark Cowell)

Chapter 10

A dogs life – hermit style

So far there have been three dogs to share my life in the islands. There was a fourth … one of the ten puppies ole' Willie fathered that time that sex came to Dismal Key, but I only had him for a few weeks so we'll say three. Coincidentally, and only coincidentally, all have been medium-sized and black. Willie even had a black tongue. In one way this has not been too good … the black part. During the summer months the tropical sun beats down like a blowtorch and black is no protection against this heat. Fortunately, dogs are sensible enough to stay in the shade … even dig a hole to find cool, moist earth for protection. They never suffered too much I am sure.

Al Seely and Digger at Everglades City Seafood Festival
(Photo courtesy of Everglades City High School students)

All three dogs were different breed mixtures. Willie had a lot of Labrador in him; Barbie was a terrier of some amalgamated strains. My present dog ... Digger ... is what? Who the hell knows? Some ole' traveling salesman type of a dog, I guess. Yet, after living with me for a year or two they all seemed to develop similar habit patterns. Different personalities, of course. But the curious thing is that I have never lifted a finger or a voice to train them in any way. It's as if they sensed what I wanted from them and were happy to oblige. I didn't even have to housebreak them.

There is one comment I should like to make here regarding the relationship between a hermit and his dog. This hermit anyway. Millions of people own dogs and I'm sure most of them could be called dog lovers; at least very devoted to their pets and seeing to their health and welfare and all. But in the average home situation ... even where the dog is part of the family ... there are some periods of separation. Kids have to go to school, parents go off to work, everyone goes to the movies, or out to a restaurant or what have you. But in my case there is no separation. My dog is with me twenty-four hours of every day ... even shares my bed at night. This, as you can guess, makes for a much closer relationship. The dog becomes a true companion and learns the significance of every move I make. So, if I sound overly sentimental about the various dogs I have had ... it's because I am.

Willie, being only a few months old when he came out here with me originally, had absolutely no experience and had to learn things the hard way through trial and error. One of his first errors, feisty little bugger that he was, was to attack a great blue heron that was more than twice his size. The heron simply turned around and gave him a couple of good pecks on the ass. End of lesson one.

He soon learned to have a healthy respect for crabs also. It was a fairly good-sized blue crab that taught him this lesson. Willie found it out on the flats and began a frenzied barking and leaping around and circling. As fast as he went around the crab circled with him, always facing him, mean-looking pincers at the ready. As you know a dog always investigated any new thing with its nose, which in this case was decidedly not a good idea. With the speed of lightning and deadly aim, the crab grabbed that inquisitive nose and hung on painfully tight until I managed to pry the claw loose. From then on Willie kept a healthy distance from all crabs.

After the first time he also kept clear of our huge, healthy, shiny cockroaches, or wood roaches, or whatever they are. Some kind of roach, certainly. His first encounter with these critters was when we were living in a tent, back on Brush Key. One was marching insolently across the tent floor and Willie went after it, snapping it up in his teeth and giving it a fling. Then, instead of pursuing his prey, he began to sneeze and shake his head violently. When he dashed outside, still shaking his head I assumed that he must have been bitten or stung. I followed him out, got him calmed down after a bit, and examined him the best I could, but could see no sign of swelling or punctures. Anyway, whoever heard of a biting cockroach? Still curious, I went back in and found the crippled bug crawling around in a tight circle. I picked it up gingerly. Then, I got it … whew … what a powerful stink! "Apparently this particular type of roach has, as a protective device, the ability to squirt some gaseous essence that is very irritating to dogs anyway.

Willie was the gentlest dog in the world when it came to people. He loved everybody … children especially. Why, he was so gentle that when I fed him tidbits by hand he simply opened his mouth and I had to place the bite in it. However, he was not kindly disposed to other dogs. He would have challenged a Great Dane, if one were handy, I do believe. At least he challenged every male dog in Goodland with fair results. And he was death on coons … literally.

I had been told before bringing him out with me that a raccoon can kill a dog. Maybe that is so. I don't know. Or maybe the coons out here are puny though they look fat and sassy enough. Anyhow, Willie ended up with a good many coon kills to his credit and only a few scars. Three of these coon-hunting stories are worth relating.

One morning just before daylight, I awoke to the sound of his insistent barking. From the special timbre of it I concluded that he had treed a coon and I turned over to go back to sleep. Before I got there, thought, I detected a different quality to his barks, more of a frantic note. I roused up then to see if I could tell where the barks were coming from. They seemed to be right out in front of the shack somewhere, which puzzled me since there are no trees there. Then, he let out a yelp, which seemed to be out off in the middle. Something was obviously wrong. I threw on my shorts and sneakers as fast as I could and grabbing my spotlight ran out to the beach to investigate. To my complete astonishment, the ruckus was coming from somewhere out in the bay and by now Willie was choking and gasping. Fortunately, the tide was out and the water shallow for a long way out. I waded out, flashing my light around until I spotted two dark forms thrashing madly in the water. When I got close enough I could see that it was indeed a coon Willie was fighting with and the coon was getting the best of it; not that it was showing superior fighting ability, it was simply not wasting its breath in frantic barking. Willie, on the other hand was trying to swim, to grab the coon by the neck, and to bark and growl at the same time and consequently was rapidly losing his strength and wind. By the time I got him away, he was fairly waterlogged, though I was much more scared than he was thinking that if I had gone back to sleep I would surely have lost one fine dog.

Dragging him by the tail back to where he could stand by himself, he choked and snorted and shook himself until he was ready to join with the enemy again. But I held him and soon picked up the rapidly swimming coon with my spotlight. It was headed for shore too, so Willie and I moved along the beach to intercept it as soon as it was close enough to dry land. Willie got his revenge with great dispatch.

There is a humorous ending to this tale. At least it tickled me. When I got Willie back to shore, Barbie was prancing around excitedly and I was curious to see how she would react to her first introduction to coon. All she did was to watch while Willie grabbed it by the scruff of the neck and shook it to death. Only then did she approach gingerly and daintily sniff the coon's rear end. Some hunting dog … that!

I should, perhaps, have told this second story first because it happened before Barbie came into my life. But since I had been talking about how coons are supposed to be able to kill dog, I thought of that one and only time when a coon almost did.

It was approaching noon on one of the hottest days of July when Willie and I were exploring the beach of a nearby island. I mention the heat because it had a definite bearing on what transpired. All of a sudden Willie darted into the brush and there were the growls and yelps of a coon fight. Usually it was only a matter of minutes before any coon that fell into Willie's clutches was neatly dispatched. This time, however, the fight went on and on until it finally seemed just to peter out. Willie didn't come trotting triumphantly back for my approval, so I decided to take a look though I wasn't too keen about pushing my way into the mosquito infest brush. Anyway, what I found was a tiny glade in there and here was Willie sprawled out on the ground on one side of it panting as if he'd burst any minute. The coon was zonked out from exhaustion on the other side. Exactly like a couple of boxers resting in their corners between rounds. As I watched, the coon began to stir around and start to get up. It never made it. Willie found some reserve of energy and went flying across the glade to hit the coon behind the head and in three vicious jerks had done it in.

In the third story the coon got away, thanks to its superior tree climbing ability. Note that I say "superior." The situation to start with was much the same as in the previous story. We were making our daily tour of Panther Beach. At least Barbie and I were on the beach. Willie was ranging along on a parallel course in the brush. Came the yelps and growls and I knew battle had been joined. Then, as in the previous stories, I detected a change in the barking from fighting barks to coon-up-in-tree barks. Then it changed to whimpers and little yips of puzzlement. Again I went into the brush to see what was going on, calling to Willie as I went. When I reached the spot where I figured the ruckus should be I could see neither coon nor dog. I called some more and then heard a replying whimper way above my head. Believe it or not, Willie was balanced on a limb no thicker than my arm at least fifteen feet in the air. The coon was perched saucily in the very tip of the tree but Willie had lost interest in it in puzzlement over how to get down from his precarious perch. I was afraid for him to jump that far so I had to climb the tree to rescue him. Once he was safely down I studied the tree trying to figure out how in hell he had managed to climb so high. The only conclusion I could reach was that an old, rotten tree trunk lying on the ground alongside must have been leaning somehow against the bigger tree to provide a sort of ladder and in scrabbling up, Willie had dislodged it and so marooned himself on that high limb. Unless he flew. Willie hung around awhile to see if the coon would be foolish enough to come down. It wasn't and didn't.

Next to his passion for hunting coons was his forever-thwarted desire to catch minnows. As smart as he was about most things, he never seemed to realize that the minnows were faster than he was. The only times he had the satisfaction of chomping into one were when the minnows were in my bait bucket. Nevertheless he spent hours leaping and splashing through the shallows after them.

Another sport at which he was much more proficient was catching horseshoe crabs. If you think this is inconsistent with my previous statement that he had learned to avoid all crabs, it can be pointed out that the horseshoe crab does not have powerful pincers. During the horseshoe crab mating or spawning season they come by the hundreds at night, the larger females (I assume) burrowing into the sand just at the water's edge, the smaller, more active males crowding around for position on the female. At such times Willie would thrust his muzzle into the water, grab one by its spiky tail and drag it up on the beach. Here he exhibited some real fancy thinking. If he simply released it, it would immediately crawl back in the water; so he had to figure out how to turn it on its back. He accomplished this by digging the sand away from one side as it moved along until he could insert his nose under the shell and flip it over. However, an overturned horseshoe crab can employ its stiff spine of a tail to right itself. Willy solved this by biting it off. I have often pondered this last refinement. It might be instinctive except that the capture of horseshoe crabs is not a natural pursuit of dogs, there being no food value in them. If it is not instinct, then it must be a high order of intelligence that enabled him to figure it all out.

You may wonder why I have detailed some of Willie's exploits and said very little about Barbie. The reason is simple enough. She never did anything worth talking about except to stay right close to me day and night. To work her way into my affections so that her death broke me up far more than the loss of Willie. That may not have been entirely due to the feelings Barbie and I had for each other. You see I knew that Willie didn't have too long to live anyway. He had heartworm. I had noticed that he began to be less energetic than usual and also plagued with a persistent cough. On one of my infrequent visits to Charlotte I had him examined by a veterinarian who diagnosed heartworm and said he might live another year or two at most. If I had had Barbie examined at the same time and found that she too was developing this dog-killer disease, I might have been spared some pain when her time came, being prepared for it. But she was so healthy and frisky, I had no suspicions that she might be a victim too.

Heartworm, I learned then is transmitted by mosquitoes and God knows there are enough of them out here. I also learned that it can be prevented by a simple medication taken daily. Digger, I don't need to say is on this regimen. I hate to think what may cause his demise. Old age, I hope.

In case you're wondering what finally happened to Willie, I can't tell you because I don't know – only that he disappeared.

When I moved to Dismal Key in 1972 I still had Willie and Barbie. About that time another hermit came out here to live in a homemade houseboat, which he had anchored in the lagoon behind my old shack on Panther Key. I haven't mentioned him because the poor old guy was not fated to live very long … not long enough to accumulate a body of anecdotes worth recounting. He had two dogs, a small German Shepherd and a little Beagle. Once when he was ill and had to go back to Fort Myers to see a doctor, he asked me to take care of his dogs for him. This I was more than willing to do, but unhappily, not successful in the doing. His shepherd and my Willie went off hunting together and were never seen again.

This was a very strange thing. I could easily visualize one dog being bitten by a rattlesnake, but not two … unless they had elected to attack it together and I was inclined to doubt that. I had seen Willie approach a rattlesnake very warily, keeping a safe distance and doing nothing but bark fit to bust his larynx. The next best guess, since I knew the dogs would swim from island to island was that a shark had gotten them. But, there again it seems unlikely that it could have gotten both dogs. I thought of bobcats. A bobcat could probably kill a dog or at least tear it up so badly that it wouldn't live long. But again, two dogs? Two bobcats, maybe?

For several days after it became apparent that the dogs were not going to show up, I cruised around the islands, stopping to whistle and call from time to time though I felt it was probably useless. Mostly, I was watching for vultures in the sky. If the snakebite theory or bobcat theory was correct, there would be carcasses somewhere to attract vultures. No vultures.

At the time I had a small vegetable garden. I am not going to bore you with an account of that fiasco, but not long after the disappearance of the dogs I did find panther tracks in the soft earth of the garden. And again I figured that a panther would be very likely to dispose of one dog, but would it try for two? And again, if a panther were responsible there would be a carcass and vultures.

The only good thing to be said for my preoccupation with the various possible fates that could have overtaken the dogs was that it kept me from being too torn up emotionally over the loss. And, as I mentioned earlier, I knew Willie had only a limited time to live anyway and it was helpful to think that maybe he had died in action.

During the succeeding weeks and months, I discussed all the possibilities with many of my friends and casual visitors. No one had any reasonable theory to suggest until one guy who owns a houseboat nearby which he uses for occasional fishing weekends asked me if possibly the crocodile had gotten them.

"Crocodile!"…I exploded. "What crocodile?"

"Didn't you know you've got a croc' down in the slough? He pointed in the direction of the slough.

"Hell," I said, "I didn't even know there was a slough back there. I thought it was just a little creek meandering up into the mangroves."

"Oh yeah. There's a good-sized slough back in there. Go and look sometime."

"But a crocodile," I pursued, "I knew there were alligators in the Everglades, but not out here. Are you sure?"

"Well", he said, "I haven't seen it, but I've heard it bellowing from my houseboat at night … and it's more likely to be a crocodile than and alligator because alligators don't hang around in salt water and crocs do."

I remembered then that in the past Willie had come back from one of his expeditions covered with mud.

"But, do you think a croc … if there is one … could have gotten both dogs?"

"Easily", he said. "If they were close to it and barking at it and all, the crock could have snapped one up in its jaws and knocked the other galley-west with its tail. Then it would have tucked both bodies down under the mangrove roots to ripen and that's why you never saw vultures around."

Well, the crocodile theory sounds as feasible as all the other theories, especially since I have myself heard the creature … whatever it is … bellowing and garumphing. But, it's another thing that no one will ever know. The two dogs were last seen trotting happily down the trail, their tails high and waggling.

I still had Barbie.

For a while.

Barbie was a different type of dog altogether. She was almost fiercely devoted to me and very affectionate – to me. But she would have nothing to do with anyone else. In fact, I had to greet all my visitors with the words: "She won't bite. Just ignore her and she'll ignore you." Well, she didn't actually ignore them. She would most likely sniff at them and growl if they tried to make overtures. But she never did bite anyone.

However, with Willie gone, I guess I did make more of her than before, petting her frequently, taking her for walks, feeding her special tidbits, and I even let her take Willie's place on my bed. So we became very close after awhile. Her death, then hit me extremely hard.

Someone had brought her a bone and after they left she was out in the front yard working on it when she started to choke. I rushed out and rammed my finger down her throat hoping to dislodge the bone fragment, which of course, I thought was the trouble. I could find nothing. I could see nothing. But she continued to choke at intervals. I tried to feed her something on the assumption that the food going down her gullet might remove the obstruction, but she wouldn't eat. She did drink a little water.

This was late on a Sunday afternoon and there was no way I could get her to a vet until the next morning. By then, she was not only continuing to choke off and on, but was very obviously ill. As soon as it was light, I got her in the boat and headed for Goodland. I went to some friends there and asked if they would be kind enough to take us to a veterinarian. They got busy right away, phoning for and appointment and trying to soothe me some. The vet gave us the earliest possible appointment but we had a couple of hours to wait before we could start out and by the time we were ready to go I had to carry Barbie out to the car.

On the way, she died.

In my lap.

We went on anyway to confirm whether she had choked to death or what. The vet examined her and said her throat was clear … she had died of heartworm. He put her body in a big plastic bag and I started home to bury her.

I got drunk and bawled like a baby all the way back in my boat.

And several times after that.

I have no hesitation in saying that it was the saddest, most horrible experience of my life.

It happened in April of 1974 and I still miss her.

As soon as I was able to function again I wrote to Charlotte asking her to find me another dog – preferably a medium-sized, short haired black dog … breed unimportant. It was six weeks before she was able to find a suitable dog and get it out to me. In the meantime, knowing how badly I felt and how lonely I must be, she bought a second-hand accordion and sent it out to me by a friend who was coming to visit. An accordion is no substitute for a living, loving dog, but it did help. Not that I can play one very well. I'm self-taught and probably don't even finger the keys and buttons properly, but in an effort to master a few tunes, I did get over the worst of my loss.

When she brought Digger, he was still a puppy, some six months old and from the moment he set foot on the island I had no more time to brood. I was too busy rescuing shoes, socks, pipes, books, and sundry other paraphernalia from his destructive playfulness.

I must say that Charlotte picked a winner though. He seems to have combined the best features of the two previous dogs. He's friendly ... loves everybody … intelligent and nearly as affectionate as Barbie. And he is also a homebody, going out in the woods only if I go, so perhaps he won't meet some unknown fate while on a hunting expedition   There is just one other thing I would like to mention that came about as the result of Barbie's demise. During the six weeks that I had no dog, the wild life hereabouts got the word that there was no longer a dog in residence and many a morning I would watch a pair of bobcats come out of the woods and wander about my front yard, coons would frolic in the old boats lying down by the dock, and the rats had a field day in the house.

Chapter 11

Shoot-out at the Shack

Every June or thereabouts, the great loggerhead turtles come ashore on sandy beaches to lay their eggs. They are protected by law, but like so many laws designed to protect wild life, enforcement is practically impossible. Anyone caught in the act of molesting one of these monsters during the actual egg-laying ritual can be fined up to $500. When you consider that the turtles come ashore only at night and further consider the miles of sandy beaches that would have to be patrolled, you can see that poaching turtles is as easy as poaching eggs.

Since Panther Key is blessed with one of the female loggerhead's favorite laying grounds, this beach becomes a prime target for the turtle hunters for at least two months every summer. It's a period I used to dread each year because the turtles have a tendency to come ashore at high tide and since high tide occurs some fifty minutes later on each successive night, and since the hunters arrive only at these times, it means that … say … on Monday night I'd be awakened around midnight by the boats roaring by with their searchlights flashing, on Tuesday it would be around one in the morning, Wednesday around two, and so on. This, to put it mildly was a pain in the ass to one who likes his solid eight hours per night.

Before I left Panther I finally got resigned to it, but during my first summer I took it all as a very personal affront. Particularly when, as sometimes happened, those guys would shear a pin on the reef and come up, get me out of bed at these ungodly hours to borrow one. Or even have the gall to ask me to make coffee for them at 3 a.m., which they never drank much of, being full of beer to begin with.

Now it sometimes happens that when I am faced with a situation involving people with whom I am unable to comfortably cope, I do the next best thing and get drunk. On the occasion of the great battle, this stupid weakness of mine could have cost me my life and may have cost Puppydup his. Puppydup was the third dog I mentioned and at the time of this incident I had only had him a few short weeks.

It was some time in the wee hours of some night or other, me sitting at my table nursing a bottle of whiskey, when a couple of boatloads of turtle hunters roared by. Shortly after, my dogs went racing out to the beach in full cry. I staggered to the door to see a group of silent men approaching my cabin.

Made both mean and bold by liquor I yelled, "Get the hell outta here! Scram! Drag your asses away from this shack!" and many other choice commands. They never broke stride nor did they reply. I yelled some more. They kept coming. Then, in my fog I recalled the many western stories I had read in which the besieged rancher steps out onto his veranda, shotgun in hand, and stops a dozen armed horsemen cold. I reached for my little .410 gauge shotgun … empty of course, and waving it around I repeated my unsavory demands that these guys go away and leave me alone.

They must have shined a light on me and seen me pointing the gun at them. At least they told me later that I was aiming it at them, though I was in no condition to know what the hell I was doing or just what did happen. All I know is that suddenly it was if the Civil War had broken out all over again.

Blam! Bloom!

A whole barrage of shotgun blasts. In my stuporous condition I thought they were simply trying to scare me. Two could play at that game I thought as I stepped back into the shack, fumbled a shell into the chamber, went out and fired it in the air.

That was a mistake. Their answering blasts were aimed at the shack if not at me. I was suddenly aware that my lamp had one out and I could hear the tinkle of broken glass. Just at this point the puppy dashed by me down the steps. I heard the crash of a gun and a yelp from the puppy. Before I could determine whether he had actually been shot or not, the vanguard of the gang rushed me, took my gun away, throwing it out in the sand and began to push me around and threaten me with all kinds of dire punishment for daring to point a gun at them. In typical drunk fashion, my bravado melted away and I begged for mercy.

The next thing I remember clearly was their rapid retreat toward their boats and me running after them sobbing about how they didn't have to shoot my dog did they?

They were gone. I got back to the shack considerably sobered, found my trusty spotlight and looked over the shambles on my table. My lamp was broken (It was a miracle that it didn't ignite when it shattered) a jar of coffee had been cut clean in two. The screen was peppered with holes – also the mattress of my cot. My bottle of whiskey had been taken, of course. Willie, who is very gun shy had taken refuge under the cot and was unscathed being below the line of fire.

I went out then to look for Puppydup, dreading what I might find. I called and tried to whistle, but I never saw him again. In the morning, despite a skull-buster of a hangover, I hunted some more for him, thinking that if he had been badly wounded he might have gone off into the nearby woods to die. I couldn't find a trace of him … no drops of blood to follow … nothing. Then a new idea occurred to me. I vaguely remembered hearing women's voices in the middle of the melee. Perhaps one of them had heard the puppy cry and sent one of the men to rescue it. I hope against hope that something like that did happen, but as far as my actual knowledge goes, the puppy simply disappeared.

In the morning … after rehash, I realized that they evidently did not mean to do me any physical harm. But I have never been able to even guess what their motive was in acting as they did. I mean about approaching the cabin so silently and menacingly. If they had shouted out in reply to my curses and said they needed something, or given me any explanation I feel sure that I would not have gone for my gun. On the other hand, once shooting began, they made sure I would not be able to follow them or rush off to register a complaint. They cut my big boat adrift, and fired a shotgun blast through the bottom of my Jon boat.

Fortunately the big boat drifted into some nearby mangroves and I was able to wade out and tow it back.

Everyone told me afterward that I would have been justified in claiming armed assault. A man's home is his castle and all that, even if it is only a shack on a deserted island. In fact, I had to be quite adamant with a couple of my friends who said that they were going to get the law on the case if I was too stupid to do so. But I insisted, and I am sure I am right, that if any of that gang had ever been brought to book for the night's escapade, revenge would have been the next order of business and my position out here in the wilderness alone is too vulnerable. A high-powered rifle would put me permanently out of the way without the tiniest clue as to who pulled the trigger.

The following summer and the one after that, the turtle hunters came as usual, roaring by at full throttle, their high powered searchlights sweeping the beach and my cabin, disturbing my sleep, scaring me half to death with the dread of another unfriendly visit. But no one came near me until the third year when a party came up to the shack all buddy-buddy even if it was two in the morning. I made coffee for them and had a chat. I didn't recognize any of them, though I doubt that I would have been able to being as drunk as I was at the time of the shooting. Nothing was said of the affair. It may have been a different gang altogether, anyway.

Not long after that my shotgun was stolen. I have not bothered to get another one.

And now, when I read about the besieged rancher stepping boldly out on his porch with his trusty shotgun in hand to stop the bad men cold in their tracks; I laugh and laugh.

Al Seely at Panther Key (March 1969)
Courtesy of Bob Steele

Chapter 12

The Painter of Panther Key[5]

Panther Key Beach by Al Seely
(Photo courtesy of Joe & Ivy Douglas)

During August of 1968, something happened that changed my entire life. I began to paint.

It all came about because July and August are bitchy months in the Ten Thousand Islands. The average daily temperature runs in the high nineties, which means that it is much higher in the blazing sun and higher still in my tarpaper-roofed cabin. Most anywhere else you could find some comforting relief in the shade or in a cool glade in the woods, but here, shade means mosquitoes. On Panther Key I had a choice, I could either stay out on the beach in the broiling sun to take advantage of the sea breeze, or I could stay in the shack and sweat. Eventually, I built a little shelter out of poles and palm fronds that I call my "'chicka-breeze" after the Seminole Indian "Chickee." There I could be fairly comfortable on hot days, but all I could think of that particular summer was to get

---

[5] In stories about the old west panthers were often referred to as painters. Thus the pun which I think is a helluva good one that I eventually painted on a sign to hang over my cabin door. Al Seely

the hell out of there for awhile, back to air conditioned civilization, cool salads, and ice cream.

I think I was also suffering some from a reaction to the first year of excitement and discovery. My life had settled into a routine and boredom was threatening. For awhile I thought I could beat the hot months by stripping to the nude, stretching out on my bunk and reading all day, but having been reared in the New England tradition that equates virtue with work, my conscience bugged me if I read all day and all night too. I felt compelled to be busy doing something. So, I went over to spend a couple of weeks with Charlotte, for comfort and also to see if I could scout up some simple hobby to pass the time when I got back.

While pawing through the odds and ends she had stacked in one closet, I came across a small box of oil paints: a beginners kit, really, with a few tubes of color, a little plastic palette and bottles of oil and turpentine. I don't remember exactly, but I think we bought that for her at some previous time when she took a short-lived interest in oil painting. Anyway, I figured, what the hell, take it back and fool with it a bit. So, I bought a beginner's book on the technique of oil painting, and a block of canvasette paper.

We've got to make a little detour here … back to very young years. My parents decided that I should become a minister of the Gospel. But, during my years in seminary I thought only of becoming a musician. I finally managed scholarships to attend the Conservatory of Music by which time I thought only of becoming an artist. Before I got sufficiently embroiled in art, to try for art school, I married my first wife. It happened that her father was a professional artist of some renown and although by then I was making fair progress in a musical career, my interest in painting got a shot in the arm. As soon as opportunity presented itself, I indicated that I would appreciate some art instruction. I was surprised and somewhat hurt when her father didn't jump at the chance to develop my embryonic talent. In fact, I had to belabor the issue before I got him to agree to make a start with me. But, one fine day he said to me,

"Well, Al, would you like to see what you can do with a paint brush?"

"Great," I cried, "When?"

"Come into the studio and we'll start right now."

He found a little end table, spread a bit of paisley drape on it in the center of which he positioned a potato. Then he took a palette, squeezed out some dollops of earth colors and white, handed me two or three brushes and said, "Have at it."

He must have seen the look of chagrin on my face as my visions of doing a Rafaelesque Madonna fizzled out like a punctured balloon. He laughed,

"Just want to see how you handle a solid shape, roundness and all that."

"Oh," I said.

In half hour or so he came over to see what I had accomplished. I held up my version of the lowly potato with some pride. I had even put eyes in it.

"No," he said sadly, "No. That's not quite it. Here, let me show you."

Whereupon he took the brush, scrabbled it in the paint and with a few swift strokes did something on the paper that looked vaguely like a potato. I thought mine was much better.

"There," he said. "Try it like that."

So I scrabbled and swift stroked like crazy. In fact, I did several of the blobs, each as near to his version as I could make it. When he looked at my work again, he was silent for some time except for some "H'mns" and throat clearings.

I might interpose here that while trying to emulate his style of painting, I had found myself involved in quite a colloquy with myself. I knew he could paint well. The house was hung with many of his beautiful canvases. He was famous. Yet, somehow I could not get away from the fact that my potato looked more like the model than his.

Then he said, "Al, I don't know quite how to say this except to say it. I'm afraid you'd do best to forget about painting."

I was furious, but what could I say ... or even think? He was the expert. I had only my egotistic notion that I could paint. The upshot was I finally convinced myself that he must be right that I had no talent.

Now ... thirty years later ... back on Panther Key, I was mixing up some color on a little plastic palette and having the unmitigated gall to try to paint a picture. At least, by God, I wasn't going to start with any potato. I was, by God, going to start right off with a masterpiece, like, for instance, my version of the Adoration of the Christ Child. Of course my version was an extreme travesty on any of the great "Adorations" of the masters.

I found in my book on how to paint a sketch of a seated female nude with a lot of lines this way and that to show the perspective of the figure. Somehow, I could visualize her with the wimple of the classic Madonna's, but with only a wisp of fabric over the figure, leaving most of her revealed. Then, in my mind's eye I saw the three wise men adoring, not the Christ child, but her. And so I painted it. At one point during the execution of it, I started to have the bare-assed child crawling away in the lower corner, but I decided that I was being sufficiently blasphemous without that added touch. When it was finished I looked at it and said to myself, "Hot dam! You can paint after all."

It is true that I had managed to place the figures in a pleasing composition under a Romanesque arch. I had portrayed the biblical-typed costumes of the wise men well enough. The perspective was appropriate at least. And using Willie for a model, the dog curled upon the stone floor provided a good touch. Yet it was obviously amateurish, even to my untrained eye.

Well ... hell. What else?

Now, some three hundred paintings later I am still an amateur though I sell pretty well. A set of art encyclopedias with fine color reproductions has given me some small idea of the work of the masters, past and present. Other books have provided information on technique and so on. And, surprisingly enough, I have had quite a number of professional artists visit me and share a nugget of constructive criticism. As a result my work has improved over the years but not enough so that I can consider calling myself an artist. Probably never will.

Lagoon Ten Thousand Islands by Al Seely
(Photo courtesy of Joe & Ivy Douglas)

As for selling my paintings; it isn't a case of their being all that good. It's mostly because they are done by a kooky hermit living on an island and because I do a lot of birds and raccoons and local seascapes. They are more in the realm of souvenir postcards than works of art.

However, I have had several fairly sophisticated people tell me that my fussy, photographic style is a relief from the abstracts and impressionistic neo-this or that daubs that still adorn the galleries. Be that as it may, the fact still remains that when anyone visits me they see only my work. I have no competition. There is no basis of comparison as there would be in an art shop where many painters are represented.

Al Seely's Foster Atkinson painting
(Photo courtesy of Bob Steele)

One other thing should be said about the sale of my work. At the very beginning if anyone expressed a complimentary interest in one of my things I'd say, "You like it? Here … take it along for a souvenir." I found I had a bit of a flair for portraits done from photographs. (If I were ever confronted with a live model I'd be struck with paralytic shock. Yeah, I would.) So then it was free portraits of my friends and their wives and such until one woman told me I should be getting some money for my work.

I was astounded. At that point in time I knew nothing about painting beyond the fact that my efforts left much to be desired. Then someone else asked what my price was for something I had done. What the Hell. Maybe I could make a buck with my new hobby. But what to charge?

If you ask enough people the same question you are apt to come up with a general answer and that is how I decided to keep my prices under fifty dollars. Which helps to explain why I am able to sell as many as I do. This isn't too dumb. Maybe now some of my painting are worth more than that, but most of the people who find their way out to my island are not likely to have two or three hundred dollars in their pockets. Many of them are just ordinary fold out for a pleasant weekend of fishing and couldn't afford that much anyway. So I get twenty-five or thirty five bucks and they get a picture they like and everyone is happy.

Sunset by Al Seely
(Photo courtesy of Joe & Ivy Douglas)

"Jiver" by Al Seely
(Photo courtesy of Joe & Ivy Douglas)

Pelicans by Al Seely
(Photo courtesy of Joe & Ivy Douglas)

I started this chapter by saying that painting changed my life, which it did in three significant ways. First it brought in some bread. I was able to further increase the quantity and quality of goodies Charlotte brought on her supply runs. Well, that's not altogether true. Oh, the increase in good grub is true enough and I went from a one-burner stove to a three and there were some other amenities that came along too. But, not much of this was due to my increased income. I did send her some money from time to time, especially if I made a multiple sale … such as having a boat-a-cade stop by and maybe selling six or eight canvases at one whackeroo. And I did manage to save over $300 to buy my present boat.

Mostly, I must admit, the money increased the amount of beer and wine I was able to buy and the gas and oil to go buy it. I rather think that is where most of the extra money went.

O. K. My conscience is clear now.

Apropos of money and booze, this following episode has never struck me as being particularly funny, but for some curious reason everyone I have told about it has roared with thigh-slapping laughter. More than that, they have passed it on to others so that occasionally I'll meet some new guy and during the introduction he'll say, "Oh, you're the guy that ended up out at Caxambas." (Caxambas is a small community south of Marco Island and about fifteen miles from Panther Key.)

It began when a friend of mine brought his brother out to visit the hermit and presented me with a case of beer. The brother was taken with some of my paintings and asked if he could bring a friend who might be interested in buying one or two. Of course I agreed.

The next day they returned with a young woman who immediately began to select some paintings she wanted to buy. I was by that time thoroughly sloshed as I worked my way through the last few cans of beer. As a result, I just sat there with an idiotic grin on my puss, watching her stack up her purchases with no idea in the world of what pictures she was selecting. Finally, she was ready and said, "Well, what do you want for the lot?"

The thought uppermost in my mind at that point was getting enough money to after some more beer, but I did have enough sanity remaining to make sure I could buy plenty, so I told her I'd like thirty-five dollars for the lot. She agreed, paid and they went off, booty in hand. I followed soon after to trek into town fro beer. Later, I discovered that she had taken eight canvases, which I would normally have charged twenty-five dollars apiece for.

Ah … the evils of drink!

Anyway, on my way to town with the thirty-five bucks burning in my pocket and still being under the influence, it seemed that the best thing I could do, would be to celebrate this good fortune with something better than beer. I bought a fifth of Johnnie Walker. I also began to sample it on the way home. Which was a mistake. Could have been a fatal mistake. For all at once I was lost. I also went into a blackout. This is a strange phenomenon peculiar to alcoholics in which you keep on doing things but never after have any recollection of what they were. So, I can't tell you what I did during the rest of that day and night, or where I went. The next thing I was aware of was waking up the next morning. I was sitting in the bottom of my boat with my head and neck hanging over one side, my legs over the opposite side. For awhile, I thought I'd never be able to move my head again, but with much groaning and cussing I finally heaved myself up onto one of the boat seats and looked around.

I was anchored in a tiny cove right plumb up against the mangroves. There was quite a bit of water in the boat which meant either that it had rained during the night or that I had fallen out of the boat and then, miraculously, been able to climb back in. I favor that explanation, as dangerous as it sounds because I was soggy wet too. Obviously, I had no idea in the world where I was.

The first thing that I tried was to yell, figuring that just maybe someone would be fishing nearby and come to my rescue. I hollered myself hoarse with no results. Then, I checked my gas can and seemed to have plenty. The motor started off easily, so I upped anchor and started off following my nose. Incidentally, I had both Willie and Barbie with me and though they seemed to look reproachfully at me, they were OK.

After winding around a few islands, I found myself coming out into the open Gulf which I recognized as a good thing, but I was still too groggy to be able to figure out which way to go to get to civilization, I just puttered along peering blearily around for some landmark. Then … joy oh joy, I spotted a channel marker and knew I was saved. I didn't recognize it but I knew it would lead me to one of three communities hereabouts. I made for it beeline and began to follow the stakes until after what seemed and eternity I saw houses. But, where? It was no place that I had ever seen before. I circled around to find a public dock, but finding none I pulled up in front of a house and went ashore. There was a road there and it seemed to go up a hill, which was strange … hills being scarce in this area. Maybe I was dreaming or hallucinating or something. To dispel this feeling of unreality I got up my courage, went to a house and rang the bell. When a woman opened the door a merest crack and peered at me suspiciously, I said,

"Please pardon me, ma'am, but I'm lost. Can you tell me where I am?" She would probably have much preferred to tell me where to go but she relented and said I was in Caxambas.

Caxambas community (circa 1920's)

"Caxambas! Christ! How in hell had I gotten way out there?" Furthermore, "How do I get from Caxambas to Goodland?" Also, by that time I was in dire need of water. So, when I got back to the house where I'd docked the boat, I summoned up my courage again and knocked on that door. This time a man answered and I asked for a drink of water. He was obliging and gave both me and the dogs a long drink of water. I asked how to get to Goodland and he said, "Just follow the stakes back until you come to the Marco River and follow that into Goodland." I thanked him, though I wasn't at all sure about that Marco River bit and started off.

About half a mile down the channel I came to what looked like a river and turned into it only to run into mud. I rowed back and forth but it was nothing but shallow, muddy water. It couldn't be the Marco River. So, back to the house for further help. That time the kindly man told me to follow the stakes until I came to Coon Key light. Ah! That was the miracle word that unlocked my memory. I knew Coon Key light. And so...

I got back to Goodland, filled my gas tank, bought another jug … all with wet money … and that time made it home to finish off my binge.

One final word. Apparently, I spent the night right where I found myself in the morning, which meant that by rights, since I was wearing only t-shirt and shorts, I should be dead, or near dead of mosquito bites. Oh yes … enough of their tiny injections of poison can kill a man. I was a mess from hundreds of bites sustained, but fortunately I had built up enough immunity over the years so that I survived. A curious thing happened though. After several months I lost all the immunity I once had. Every mosquito bite became an itching, raw bump. And my bruised neck was sore for a week.

Well, that's the story that people think is so funny.

Back to painting and the changes in my life.

The second change came about more gradually. It was simply that as people came and bought paintings from me and showed them to their friends, the friends came to look, sometimes to buy. These folks told others about the hermit who was also an artist and by word of mouth and some little publicity in a local newspaper my status changed from just being a hermit to becoming a regular tourist attraction, complete with guest book which now shows an average of seven or eight hundred visitors per year.

The most important change, however, was that painting filled a need in my life. As I said, the novelty of living on an island had worn off after a couple of years and I had to find a stabilizing interest.

A hermit would go nuts if he didn't always have something to do, even a phony hermit.

Chapter 13

How's the Fishin'?

Gomez's water barrel near Gomez Point on Panther Key

People are always asking, "How's the fishin'?" or some version of it like, "Where are all the fish at?" or "Catchin' any big ones lately?" If they ask where are all the fish at, I promptly point back into the jungle and say, "They went that away." For any other form of the question I put on my best hermit drawl and say, "Well, I'll tell ya. After fishin' as much as I have over the past ten years or so I've learned just one thing…(suitable pause for suspense)…fish are where ya find them."

And that, truly, is the core of my fishing knowledge.

Of course I have leaned a couple of peripheral things like the fact that hereabouts a fish no longer seem to travel in schools but in groups of one. School dropouts, maybe?

I've also learned that it all depends on who's doing the fishing, as you can see from the following story.

As long as I lived in my shack on Panther Key I kept hoping that I could walk directly out to the beach, pick up a fiddler crab to bait my hook, cast it into the water right at that spot and catch something besides catfish, which aren't worth anything … the saltwater variety anyway. I never did. I always had to walk way the hell down the beach to the cove or reefs. Naturally, I assumed that the reason I never caught anything in my front yard, so to speak, was that there were no fish there to catch. Until the day a boat anchored just offshore there and two guys started fishing.

I like to be helpful whenever I can so I strolled down to the beach to tell these misguided folks that they were wasting their time. Before I got to hailing distance I saw one guy's rod flip into a tight arc and the tip began to oscillate. Catfish, I figured. Imagine my surprise when he hauled in a nice fat trout. Just then the other guy caught one. I watched with my big mouth hanging open while they took in eight or nine beauties. The next day I fished the hell out of that spot … three catfish!

Another bit of fishing wisdom I can pass along is that if you want to take home a trophy winner be sure to bring along your kids to catch it.

This truth was revealed to me when a party spent a weekend in Roy's abandoned houseboat on the tiny island in the middle of the bay. I don't recall the exact family delineations, but there were three men and three kids around ages of six or seven, maybe younger or a hair older. Damn if I know. Little kids, anyway.

During the hottest part of the second afternoon, the men brought the kids over to Panther and turned them loose. They explained that they were sick and tired of fishing, having no luck and wanted to relax over their beer. They asked me if I would be kind enough to wave a white cloth if by any chance one of the kids got hurt or something, and they'd come over immediately. I agreed but I assured them that it had been my observation that kids led some kind of charmed existence the way they can fling fishhooks and plugs around without ever looking what they're doing and yet never lose an eye or anything.

Some time later Willie's barking called my attention to one of the kids coming up the beach as fast as he could pump his short legs.

"Hey, will ya wave a cloth for my daddy?" he panted.

"What happened?" I wanted to know, fearing that maybe the charm had suddenly lost its power.

"We got a Snook too big to carry," he said pointing back the way he had come. Here were the other two tikes tugging and dragging a fish almost as big as themselves.

I hated to put a scare on the fathers but I waved the white cloth and they came barreling across at full throttle. "When they saw the Snook, they rushed back for their rods to try their luck in the same spot. I wandered on down an hour or so later to see how they were doing. The kids had caught two smaller Snook … the parents, nothing. The big one weighed in at 18 pounds, incidentally.

The next fish story illustrates a point that is probably only valid as it applies to me. It doesn't pay to break the law. The law in this case being the one, which states that, you can only catch mullet with a gill net, in this state anyway.

The lagoon behind the shack was a favorite hangout for huge mullet. At low tide when the water is not too deep you could see them swimming lazily around …and I mean around. When I said how crazy mullet were I forgot to add that they often swim in circles, nose to tail, like pinwheels.

Watching some of them like that one day with my mouth watering, I thought, "To hell with the law, I'm going to get me one of those bastards," and I went for my bow and arrow. I wasn't really concerned about breaking the law … that would be nothing new … but I was concerned about my bow and arrows, because it didn't have a bow fishing reel attachment and I hated to lose an arrow. I figured that with the water so shallow if I were fortunate enough to hit one I'd simply wade in and grab it by the tail.

I hit one all right. On the first shot. But, before I could blink an eye it was gone … arrow and all. It didn't seem that it could get very far with a 28-inch arrow stuck in it somewhere. So, as soon as the tide came in some I put my Jon boat in the water and began to row around hunting for it. No luck.

The next day at low tide I went out to see if by some rare chance I could spot my arrow. And there it was stuck into some mangrove roots on the far side of the lagoon. There was no fish attached to it though. The mullet had apparently figured out how to wedge the arrow in the roots and work itself free. At any rate the arrow could be retrieved simply by wading across and getting it. About halfway there I took a step forward and found myself up to my thighs in quick-mud. I tried to pull my left leg free, but the only thing that happened was that my right leg sank a few inches deeper. I pulled on the right leg and the left one sank some more. After a couple of these futile attempts I stopped to consider the situation and it was far from hopeful. I was too far from the opposite shore to reach a mangrove branch to pull myself out with. There were no boats around. No one to whom I could call for help. It struck me that of all the ways a guy could get dead out here, dying of thirst while stuck in the mud would hardly be my choice.

I had no idea why I did then exactly what I did but I have since learned from a native of these parts who had been in a similar jam himself that it was the right thing. In desperation I threw myself flat in the mud and scrabbled like a dog digging a bone until I could clutch some firmer terra and pull myself slowly free.

Since then I have had a tendency toward lawfulness.

For a guy who has fished as much as I have, it is remarkable how few fish dinners I've consumed as a hermit. I think fishing is simply too complex for me to master. You see, if the tide, temperature, wind speed and direction, barometric pressure, position and phase of the moon, and the salinity of the water are all favorable, and if you fish in the morning, evening, or at night; use the right bait or plug; jig or other lure; keep pure thoughts in your mind, and hold your mouth right … you'll likely end up with a fat fillet in the skillet.

Obviously I'm neglecting one of these vital factors.

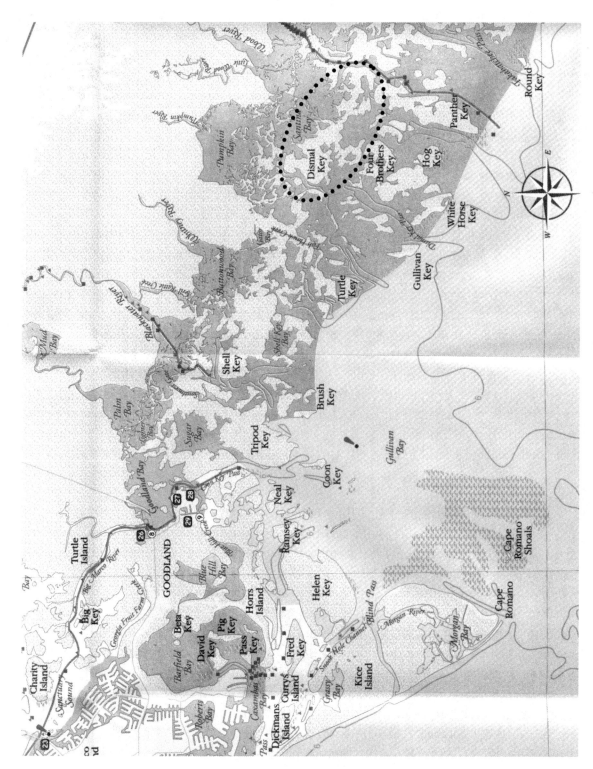

Dismal Key

Chapter 14

Back to Dismal Key

On Saturday afternoon, May 20, 1972, I found myself standing in the main room of the Dismal Key house surrounded by boxes and bags of all my worldly possessions crammed in around and on top of all the possessions, of the recently deceased Foster. All his worthless possessions, that is. The few things of value he had owned were removed by his daughter who had come out from Texas for his funeral.

If I didn't cuss and groan, I should have. I was here to stay and it didn't seem possible even to clear a footpath from the front door to the kitchen let alone making the house comfortably livable.

I am tempted to compare the Herculean task that was before me to the cleaning of the Augean stables – but for two things. Hercules had a thirty-year accumulation of shit to dispose of in one day whereas I had only a fourteen-year accumulation of junk and plenty of time to clear it out. The other thing is that I despise writers who lard their works with classical, poetical, and other learned references to show how smart they are.

How come I'm smart-ass enough to know about the Greek legend of Augeas?

I looked it up in the Encyclopedia. That's how come.

Oh well, I did know what to look for, but damned if I know how I knew. Some dim schoolboy memory, maybe?

Assuming that your memory is better than mine, (when I get to the end of a book I can never remember how it began) you may wonder why earlier in this account I eulogized Foster's three-room, split-level, waterfront home, with all its fascinating furnishings and strange knick-knacks, and now I am referring to it as a house crammed full of junk. Just so. But nearly six years had elapsed since my first impression of it and during that time poor old Foster had gotten progressively weaker until he was barely able to walk across the room. During his declining years it is doubtful that he ever lifted a finger to keep his house in any kind of order or cleanliness. So, for the first week of my residence I spent the daylight hours in endless trips to the junk pile carrying out things like cans of bent and rusty nails, boxes of old nuts an bolts, obsolete motor parts, wire, bottles, empty tin cans, boxes full of sea oat grass for basket making, boxes of yarn for knitting, bags of scraps of rags for rug making, bottles full of buttons, pounds and pounds of modeling clay, armload after armload of desiccated paper-back books and ancient magazines. Old newspapers, ragged blankets and a closet full of moldy, roach infested clothes; to say nothing of broken chairs, and the three double-decker bunks with their filthy mattresses, which wouldn't burn worth a damn … just smoldered and stunk up the yard for a couple of days.

Yeah, I know. Those things were the very element of Foster's life. The magical paraphernalia he used to ward off the evil eye of boredom; and because I liked Foster, this was a somewhat painful procedure. I had to keep telling myself that this was my home now and I should arrange it to suit my needs. So, everything went except the usable furniture; table and straight chairs, two easy chairs, a double bed I decided to use for myself, and two old day beds and mattresses for overnight guests.

I kept two souvenirs … no, three. Foster took up painting and drawing shortly after I did. I kept his sketchbook, which has some really first-rate work in it considering that he had passed seventy years of his life with the belief that he couldn't draw a straight line. I also kept a small paintbrush he had made. To the end Foster was survival conscious and after he began to paint even though he had purchased a fine set of materials, he got to wondering what would happen if he were unable to buy paint brushes for some reason and so devised a usable brush from a sea-oat stalk, split at one end were he inserted a tuft of hairs cut from his dogs tail and bound tightly with thread. The third souvenir is a ball of twine. Yards and yards of twine made from the fibers of the Spanish bayonet plant, which abounds here.

The work of settling in was considerably hampered by the fact that I was swamped with visitors during the first weeks. The word had gotten around that Ol' Foster was dead and many ghoulish types came hoping to poke through the remains in search of anything valuable. Some of these were chagrined to find me already in residence, others went ahead anyway and sorted through the junk I had pitched out.

In one instance this proved a case of my loss being another's gain. Foster had for years used an ancient Franklin stove to heat his main room, but when I took over I found a crack in the firebox and concluded that it was not safe to use. I, like an idiot, pitched it out in the dump. Someone, I forget who it was, spotted it and asked if I had any plans for it. I said I had already done what I intended to do with it. Too late, I realized my mistake as they went lugging it down to their boat, chatting merrily about its possible worth as a valuable antique. Oh well.

Other folk came because they had found my old shack on Panther Key vacant and were curious about my new status. All in all, I was a pretty popular hermit for a while.

The process of making the Dismal home livable included a few major enterprises, which I could not have accomplished by myself. So it is time to introduce a new character into this chronicle … one Nelson B. or Nels, as we all call him.

Nels Barlow

Nels is a man about my age and he has a beard, but there is where any comparison stops. He is one of a vanishing, if not extinct breed of men. I fancy there may have been men like him back in the pioneering days, men who were willing to help their neighbors under any conditions with absolutely no thought of personal gain. Sounds weird in the context of our self-centered, dog-eat-dog society today doesn't it? True. I think Nels would cut short a trip to the bathroom in order to give anyone a hand. Beyond this, he is a most ingenious fellow when it comes to anything mechanical or with anything that needs to be built or repaired. He keeps a wonderful homemade houseboat anchored across the channel from my place, which he uses for frequent weekend fishing trips.

Nelson's Houseboat Seasah at Dismal Key
(Photo courtesy of Bob Steele)

When he found out that I was moving in on Dismal he came around and started a whole program of improvements for me ... things I would never even have thought of doing. For instance, the old house had a considerable forward tilt where the pilings had settled into the ground over the years. He showed up one weekend with hydraulic jacks and cement blocks and with a modicum of assistance from me, he leveled it.

The cistern was pretty much of a mess. He brought a power unit, pump, mortar, sand, and mortar paint. Directly, I had a shining, clean, white cistern.

Foster's old dock was so rickety it was unsafe to use. Nels brought several boatloads of timbers and other lumber and huge bolts, and then proceeded to build a brand new dock after demolishing the old one. He salvaged the pecky-cypress planks for flooring.

He noticed that there was no really good place for me to paint because all of the windows in this old house are small. Out comes a great big window with

louvered panes and as I steadied the ladder and handed him tools he cut out a hole in the north wall and installed it.

Then came the business of mowing an acre of waist-high weeds around the house. Nels brought his power mower, and with some tinkering, got Foster's old brush mower farting away and we did that job together.

All of this and more with no thought of compensation from me.

What a friend to have!

Nels Barlow

Cutting Trails

Later there was a matter of cutting trails. I imagine that by now anyone might wonder what in merry hell this trail-cutting business is all about. Everywhere I go I cut trails. No, it's not a mania actually. Perhaps I can explain.

On my first island I cut trails out of pure curiosity. I wondered what might be found in the interior of the tiny island and the only way to find out was to cut a way in. On Panther Key at high tide one could not walk around to the opposite side of the island via the beach. Hence a cross-trail was indicated. Soon I discovered that visitors, especially tourists from up north were fascinated by the interesting nature walks over these trails with me pointing out things of interest and spouting off what little I know about flora and fauna. On Dismal Key, trails for the delight of my visitors are almost essential because it is the only way people can see some of the things that make this a fascinating island.

There was another reason for the main trail. I mentioned the cabin located on the back end of the mound where the owners come for their fishing weekends. Part of the deal of my living here has to do with checking on that cabin periodically, setting out rat poison and so on. It can be reached by boat, of course, but the half-mile or more trail makes a good walk for Digger and me aside from the conducted tours.

Foster had neglected the trail for years and in this part of the country if you neglect a trail, lawn, or anything else for even a couple of months, the jungle takes over. So, I had my work cut out for me opening it up again.

With the machete and then the mower I began hacking away at it a few yards each day until I suddenly realized I had lost it. I came up against a solid wall of Dildoe cactus and impenetrable vines. Dildo cactus is something else again. It grows in the same manner as prickly pear cactus with which you may be familiar; that is, each leaf or pad or what have you grows out of the preceding one. Whereas ordinary pear cactus has thin, fluted branches up to fifteen feet in length, these branches growing each out of the end of the preceding ones makes this monster into a veritable fence, with the branches intertwining and thickly tangled. Like most cacti, the pines or needles are fierce. Cutting dildo cactus can be hazardous to your health, your hands, arms, and legs.

After hacking my way a yard or two into this mass in four or fine directions without finding any hint of the old trail I was ready to give it up as a bad job. But one day a young man came to visit who had been coming here over the years to visit Foster and he was certain he could find the way through for me.

Two of Mr. Seely's many visitors Brett Stokes and Buddy Brown
(Photo courtesy of Everglades City High School students)

We armed ourselves with machetes and set out. This man was formidable. He took the lead and whacked his way like a demon this way and that, stopping periodically to climb a tree to get his bearings and forging out again in some new direction.

I have got to go back a bit to give this story its punch. There is an old cistern somewhere near the center of this mound, which we call the middle cistern. I'll have more to say about that later on, but when this guy and I started out trail hunt we had already passed the middle cistern. I had previously found my way that far.

Anyhow, after an hour or two of sweaty, back breaking work during which we must have traversed at least a mile, we broke in to a clearing and behold – the middle cistern. I had often heard or read of people being lost in the woods going in circles, but that was my first experience of it. It was a strange feeling to be so completely baffled by vegetation.

The upshot of the whole matter was that when I told Nels about our experience he, as usual, came up with a workable solution. He went around by boat to the back shack with a portable bullhorn. As he worked into the trail from that end, I approached from my end and by following the sound of his calls I was finally able to break through the thickest part of the dildo-jungle wall and find the rudimentary trail again on the other side.

The Trail

Having done all this yakking about trails, the least I can do now is to give you a tour over the trail to the back shack. Perhaps you can imagine that you are part of a group of tourists about to go over it with me.

We gather in the back yard while I get my stick … a six-foot, very stout staff. This is for the purpose of flushing out and killing any rattlesnakes that might be lurking near the path. Fortunately, the only times I have encountered snakes along the trail I have been alone. I fancy that a group of people talking and laughing and the tramp of many feet sends the snakes slithering to safety. As for the stick, I would undoubtedly look more impressive carrying my rifle or wearing my revolver in my belt, but the fact is that Digger is so gun shy that if I ever had to use either gun he would rush off into the jungle and stay hidden for ten or twelve hours. Anyway, the stick is just as lethal.

Before we start off, I call attention to what I call my medicine garden … a large, rambling bed of aloe plants. Whether these are native or were planted by some earlier resident, I don't know, but the gooey, gummy substance in the thick succulent spikes is the greatest specific for sunburn or burns of any kind that can be found … Coppertone not-withstanding. In fact, Florida has a huge cosmetic industry based on this substance … Aloe-Creme products. Somehow tourists from the North seem to feel that the proper attire for a boating expedition to fish or go sightseeing is abbreviated trunks for the men and bikinis for the women … plus sunglasses. Time and again I have had people so dressed show up here with an ugly red already showing on their customarily protected white skin. I not only show them the plants and describe the healing properties, but often slice a few stalks and give them a treatment.

Shading the aloe bed is a satin-leaf bush. This is usually something which delights the newcomers because the leaves are a glossy deep green on the upper side and a satiny brown on the under side. It has another interesting feature. The fruit, little berry-like things can be chewed and though they have no particular flavor they do have the peculiar faculty of becoming exactly like chewing gum after awhile.

We now string out in single file and enter the trail, which in many places looks more like a tunnel through the jungle growth. A few steps brings us to a Key Lime tree on one side of the trail and a false mastic tree on the other side. Nearly everyone has heard of key lime pie but not everyone has seen the thorny tree on which the limes grow, so it is of some interest. Practically no one has heard of the false mastic tree, which is not to be wondered at as it is of no particular interest except that it does bear a small yellow fruit that is edible if not very delectable.

The rest of the walk might be more interesting if I were able to name all the different trees, shrubs and plants along the way. Then again, it might be an awful bore. At any rate I can identify only a very few and have so far not been seized with any desire to learn the rest.

Next comes the rotting remains of the old chicken house which is different from some others in that the individual coops were built six feet off the ground and all the surrounding trees have sleeves of tin on the trunks ... precautions to keep the wildcats and coons from free chicken dinners.

Just behind the chicken house I point out a wild papaya tree and explain some of its possible uses such as I have described back in Chapter Four. Except that I forgot to mention that smoking the dried leaves is supposed to relieve asthma; and that fresh leaves wrapped around meat for a few hours will tenderize it. A versatile plant.

Then we come to a hole, weed grown now, but in which one can still see a couple of rotting timers. This, I say, goes back to the early 1960's when, if you recall, we were very much concerned with the possibility of Russia dropping atomic bombs on us. Foster, true to his unflagging survival instincts, proceeded to begin to build a fall-out shelter on the assumption that a bomb dropped on Miami or Homestead Air Force base or military installations at Tampa or elsewhere might cause radioactive fallout over Dismal Key. He never finished it because once you get below the level of topsoil and hit the basic shell construction of the island mound, the digging is next to impossible. I imagine that by the time he had his main hole started and began to put in some timbers the bomb threat had diminished or else, like most of us hermits, his laziness prevailed and he figured to hell with it. In any event the labor was not altogether wasted because he found that he had dug into what he referred to as a "midden," an area rich in potsherds and Calusa Indian shell tools.

A few yards beyond the fallout shelter I point to a scraggly bush with slender leaves that twice a year has a crop of tiny red peppers. I have a few hardy or foolhardy souls who collect them to use for seasoning, but they are hot beyond all imagining.

Then we come to my dig, a hole some five or six feet in diameter where I occasionally add to my collection of Indian artifacts. I have a sturdy sieve and the procedure is to dump a shovelful or two of dirt into this sieve, bash it back and forth until the soil goes through leaving a residue of shells and possibly shards or tools. The sifted soil goes into one pile and after I have picked out the goodies the shells go in another pile. The reason for this separation of the residue is that the soil is very rich and some folk have been glad to cart it off by the bucketful to enrich their lawns and gardens.

It is the very spot from the standpoint of artifacts. Every shovelful will turn up a few pottery fragments but most of these are of no particular interest except, perhaps to a dedicated archaeologist. I have left a pile of these pieces along the path for my visitors to paw over and help themselves to as souvenirs. Every fourth, sixth, or tenth shovel will turn up a shard with a design incised on it, or a rim piece, or one with a bail hole, or maybe a tool or fish vertebrae or small animal bones. These I keep for my collection, which I will describe when we get back to the house.

Immediately surrounding my potsherd hole is a lush growth of a plant with succulent stems and leaves, which is known variously as Life Plant, Cathedral Bells, Live-forever, Floppers, or Air Plant. Actually it is the *Pryophyllum* species of Kalanchoe. On a recent visit to Charlotte over in Hollywood I was browsing through some seed catalogues she had and whooped with glee and amazement when I found an ad which offered two leaves of the above plant for something like a dollar and a half. "My God," I cried, "if I could get just one penny for every two leaves of that plant I'd be a rich man." Which is no exaggeration. My island is carpeted with it. In fact it is one of the more common weeds throughout south Florida. So how come anyone would offer the leaves for sale at such an exorbitant price? Well, it is a very unusual plant. You can take a leaf and pin it to a curtain or put it on a shelf and forget about it. Within a couple of weeks, tiny roots will appear at the notches, which surround the leaf and later baby plants will grow. No soil, no water, no anything. It's like magic.

I usually give a few of these fabulous leaves to everyone who stops here, but I always give them a warning too. The plant is so hardy that once it gets a start in your garden it is practically impossible to control or get rid of. Its only redeeming feature, aside from its marvelous reproductive capacity is that it does have a rather pretty bloom … clusters of reddish-lavender bells on a tall stalk.

Just beyond the dig is my sapodilla tree. It's a large tree and in season bears a brownish-skinned fruit that is quite tasty. I usually gather a few each year to show people or to eat myself though I am not overly fond of them. The coons eat the rest.

Now, as we go along, I call the visitor's attention to the Jamaica Dogwood trees and set them searching along the high branches for tree snails. I have not been able to get hold of much information about these colorful creatures except to learn that they are fairly rare in this area. When Foster lived here he had so many people coming to collect them that they became almost extinct on Dismal Key and he finally put a stop to it. However, in the last few years they have made and excellent comeback and there are hundreds of them around now. They are collector's items mainly because of their pretty shells that have a great variety of color patterns, bands of yellow and brown and tan and black spiraling around the graceful conical shells.

Now the trail begins to go down a rather steep declivity. This usually calls forth a comment or two from people who have come to think of south Florida as being very flat. One of the unusual features of this shell mound is that it is mostly a series of hills and valleys. Here comes another mystery. Obviously the Indians constructed these hills and valleys for some reason. If there was a level area on top of beach hill one could conjecture that they placed their huts or wickiups or whatever the hell kind of shelters they lived in on the top of these hills to provide drainage or a look-out to see what their neighbors were up to. But the tops are invariably rounded off on all sides. One so-called expert insisted that the natives built a chickee-like platform with thatched roof and with a hole in the center of the floor. As they ate their endless meals of shellfish, they tossed the shells into the holes and in this manner the mounds were created. Yeah. I can't say for sure he is wrong.

At the bottom of the hill we have been going down we find a rather large clearing and in it the aforementioned middle cistern. From the way this cistern is constructed and the poor rough quality of the concrete used, it is quite obviously older than the one near my house, which provides me with water. Logs were used instead of boards to build the form into which the concrete was poured, shoveled, or what have you. The imprint of those logs is still visible. It is customarily at least half full of greenish, slimy water and the reason this water is not clean and fresh and sweet as is the water in my cistern is that there is no roof over it to keep out the sunlight. A few rotted boards and a piece or two of corrugated tin nearby would indicate that it had a roof at one time. In fact, I have been told that one of the early settler families on Dismal used it for laundry purposes. Some ancient Clorox bottles scattered around would bear this out.

One thing has always puzzled me about this cistern and that is its location. Bear in mind that this is an island and you'll agree that anyone who lived here a hundred years ago had to come and go by boat just as I do today. My house and its cistern are located only a few yards from the water, and the back shack with its cistern is right on the water too, but this middle cistern is a long hike from water in any direction. It beats me why anyone would have chosen a location like that. It has been suggested that whoever lived there (and I have never been able to get even a clue to the identity of the middle cistern residents) might have had a moonshine operation requiring the water supply. Who knows? I probably never will.

There is just one other item of interest concerning this cistern ... my frustrated fig tree. One of the native trees in these parts is the Strangler Fig. It is so named because often a seed will germinate on another tree and the seedling will send out roots, which will eventually strangle the host tree. One corner of the cistern has a Strangler Fig against it. Its roots spread around two sides, poking into any cracks and chinks. It is obviously doing its damndest to strangle the cistern.

The trail now winds up again, and up some more to the top of the highest mound on the island. Actually, it is only some eighteen feet above sea level but for this part of the country that is high, man.

It leads down now, more gradually and winds around past a thorn tree known as a sweet acacia and comes direct to that lousy dildo cactus-jungle wall I told about, which I have to keep working on incessantly to stay ahead of the rapid growth of the vines and cacti.

Past this area opens up a bit, not a meadow exactly, but a region of small shrubs and many medium-sized guava trees. Unfortunately, there is something wrong with these fruit trees. Seven or eight years ago I went out with Foster and gathered a bushel of plump, yellow guavas with no sweat and he made delicious jelly from them, but now, one or two shriveled guavas to a tree is par.

Past this sterile orchard, we come to a portion of the trail where the trees and bushes are festooned with a lichen that resembles Spanish moss except that it is of a much finer texture. Some of the records kept by the Spanish explorers tell of the Calusa Indians as being tall, comely, and very warlike. They also described the garb of the women as consisting of skirts made from some plant fibers. I have no proof, but it seems logical that they were made from this soft, pliable lichen.

A few yards further on I point to a clutch of sticks and twigs some two and a half feet across in the top of a gumbo-limbo tree. This is an osprey or fish hawk nest. I first became aware of it one day when I found a fair sized fish lying in the path near the tree. I might mention that the reason I saw the fish on the path and didn't see the nest in the top of the tree is that due to snakes I have a tendency to watch the ground around me rather than sky gaze. Naturally, I puzzled over the fish, wondering how in the hell it got there. Then, I heard the familiar peep-peep of an osprey, and looking up saw the nest.

Across from the gumbo with the nest is a Royal Poinciana tree, which means that around the next bend we will see the back shack. There is another log-ribbed cistern here, which is evidence that someone lived here too some hundred years ago more or less.

Well, that's the trail with its high spots. There are of course many little things of interest for the observant tourists, several kinds of air plants or bromeliads, globs of grey and gold ball moss, varicolored flat lichens, myriad birds, slithering anoles (locally called chameleons), an occasional shell tool fragment lying in the path, and sundry animal droppings.

Back at the house I get out my wooden tray of artifacts for inspection. It is not an impressive display, due primarily to the fact that my enthusiasm for digging and sieving only manifests itself at rare intervals and for periods of short duration. But it is fairly representative, I think, of the types and kinds of artifacts to be found on Dismal Key. One of the things most people notice at first glance is the variety of designs on the shards, ranging from a simple single line just below the rim to fairly complex designs incorporating several different motifs.

Over the years I have had many visitors who are supposedly knowledgeable about Calusa artifacts. Some are simply enthusiastic amateurs, but others have indicated university affiliation or said that they were professional anthropologist. I don't ask for credentials and I give them all my sincere attention, but I can't avoid a certain skepticism when I encounter so many conflicting theories, or theories that seem illogical to me. The decorated potsherds are a case in point.

One guy, I recall, went through my collection like a woman picking over undies on a bargain table. He would pounce on a fragment and say, "Oh, this is from the … tribe 150 A.D." Another would be from the … tribe at some later century. Still another fragment was from an earlier period and so on. Finally, I asked him, "Well, how come I found all these specimens in a hole not more than six feet in diameter?" He countered quickly with the theory that since Dismal Key is one of the larger Indian mounds hereabout it was likely that the various tribes gathered here for conclaves, festivities and sundry other orgies. Since it does seem to be an accepted fact that these superstitious Indians destroyed their pots after using … much like the Russians smashing their wine goblets … the variety in tribal designs would be thus accounted for.

But, I am not satisfied. Somehow, I can't visualize the members of twenty or thirty tribes smashing their pots and scattering the shards in such a small area. Furthermore, if that was what happened, I'd find several fragments bearing each of the various designs. Which is not the case. Usually I never find more than two pieces with the same design. So, what happened to the rest of the pot?

Anyhow, regardless of how they got there, I have found in that one small area a great variety of designs and some variety in clay textures: smooth, rough, stained with color, fire-blackened, and so on. I also have one or two sandstone tools of some sort, several kinds of shell tools, and some shell beads or pendants. None of my experts have ever told me that the fish and animal bones I find are remnants of Calusa meals, but maybe my guess in the matter is as good as theirs.

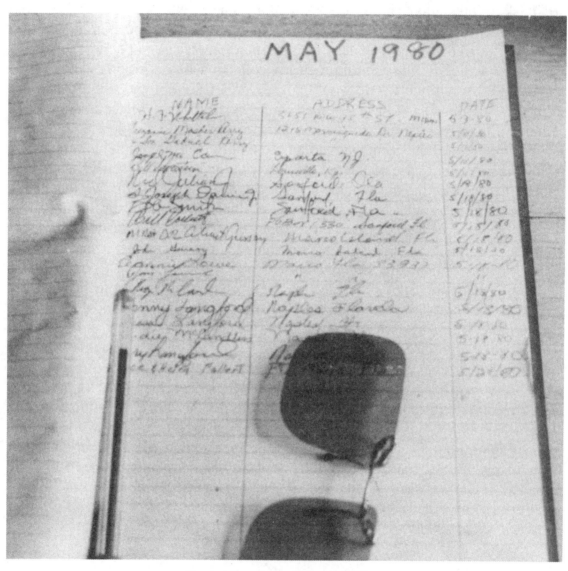

Guest book at Dismal Key
(Photo courtesy of Everglades City High School students)

Chapter 15

Potpourri of Visitors

Life on Dismal Key has not been any different for me with respect to the number and variety of visitors who come here. I did start a guest book for them to sign and from it I ascertain that an average of six to eight hundred people visit here each year. But, I imagine that if I had kept records on Panther Key I would have found a similar number.

The fun of having a guest book is in seeing how many different states and towns and cities are represented, as well as foreign countries. I also have signatures of several celebrities. There are a couple of interesting stories about celebrities, but since I mentioned foreign countries before I mentioned celebrities, let me tell you about a group of tourists from Cologne, Germany.

One of the charter boats brought them. The captain told me where they were from and asked if they could come up and look at my paintings and see how a hermit lived. I welcomed them and began to tell them about this being an Indian mound and so on until I discovered that only one of them could speak English and not very well at that. From then on I let him ask questions to which I gave the simplest replies possible, which he then translated for the others.

I said earlier that I detest writers who use a lot of foreign phrases and quotations in their work. But in this case my ability to understand and speak a few rudimentary German phrases makes the story.

As we came along up the path I was able to pick out a word here ... a phrase there even though German as spoken by natives is a far cry from textbook or classroom German. In fact, I very much wished I had a better command of the language when we got to the house and they began to discuss my paintings. It was very frustrating not to know whether they were praising them or laughing at them.

Finally, after one exchange the interpreter asked if any were for sale. I assured him they were all for sale. Which one did they have in mind?

Let me digress here just a bit to explain that I have what I consider my best paintings framed and displayed on the walls. My lesser works are stacked up on the floor. One of the group had been looking through this stack and had taken one out and propped it on a chair for better viewing. His choice quite surprised me because it was a landscape I thought so little of that I had never even signed it. That, however, was the one he wanted to buy. The next question, naturally, was how much. I said I'd be happy to get ten dollars for it. The interpreter turned to the would-be purchaser and said, "Zehn dollar" ($10).

Immediately one of the women in the group cried, "Nichts zehn dollar ... zu viel, zu viel! Sieben oder acht ist genug." By which I understood her to mean that ten dollars was too much. Seven or eight was enough.

That burned my ass. Ordinarily I get up to thirty-five dollars for my paintings. Ten buck was a ridiculous bargain and they were still trying to beat me down. Poker-faced I repeated my ten-dollar figure.

After another spate of gutturals and gestures the interpreter indicated that the man would take it. Then there ensued a real comedy routine as they passed money back and forth and dug in pockets and argued until finally they handed me a tightly wadded bunch of bills. I quickly spread them out and counted them. Five singles! I really burned then. I tapped the purchaser on the shoulder and in my best classroom German I said, "Nichts funf dollars- ZEHN dollars."

Talk about dropping jaws. It was worth the whole cheating shebang just to see the expressions on that group of faces when they realized that I knew some German and had possibly understood their whole denigrating scheme. Let me tell you they hustled up the other five dollars in a flash and away they went, grumbling and muttering ... barely able to take their leave gracefully.

Another time a charter boat brought a group of men to look over the hermitage. I got down to greet them just as they came along the dock, a tall, beefy man in the lead. Before I had a chance to introduce myself and find out who they were and where from and so on, this big guy pointed to Foster's old fiberglass boat ... a Sears Ted Williams Game fisher ... which was lying upside down in the weeds nearby, and in a voice as huge as his body said,

"Hey. How do you like that cute little boat?"

Having an unfortunate tendency to be honest I replied, "Frankly, it ain't worth shit."

Everyone seemed to think this was hilarious and while they were grouped about the big guy, slapping him on the back and guffawing, the charter captain pulled me to one side and said, "For God's sake don't you know who that is?"

I didn't. So in an almost reverent voice he told me,

"That's Ted Williams."

You can understand that the only thing I wanted to do at that moment was to run behind the boathouse and curl up in the bushes for an hour or two. But I noticed that the great man seemed to be as amused as everyone else ... and I had only spoken the plain truth after all. We shook hands and were introduced and nothing more was said about the cute little boat.

The rest of the story is anti-climactic but may serve to point up my basic naiveté. After he and the others had signed the guest book, admired my paintings and asked the usual questions about how I manage without refrigeration and how I got my supplies and so on, Ted Williams asked me how I was fixed for fishing gear. Did I need any lures, jig, plugs, or other paraphernalia? I thanked him kindly but said I was Ok, that I didn't fish much anyway. He kept asking me if I was sure. Wasn't there something in the fishing line I could use? His insistence puzzled me some but I maintained that I didn't need anything. As they went out, the charter captain got me aside again and told me in so many words that I was a damn fool. It seems that part of Ted's role as sponsor of Sears' sporting goods is to hand out free samples of all kinds of fishing gear. I had just missed a chance to get a fine haul of lures, swivels, hooks, or what have you.

Ted must have come to the conclusion that I was a pretty sad article because the next day he made a special trip back here to give me a stack of Sports magazines. He was determined that I should have something to remember him by … as if my original embarrassment about the little boat wasn't sufficient.

I have on one wall an autographed picture of Don Shula, head coach of the world-famous Miami Dolphins. Everyone spots it and asks if Don was out here to visit me. Regretfully, I tell them he wasn't but I regale them with the story about how I did happen to get his picture. It was this way:

Three or four years ago I had for a short time a German shepherd dog named "Shula." At least that is what I understood the name to be. One day in a group of tourists one man introduced himself as Dave Doroucek who was a former Dolphin player now involved in the TV broadcasting of the Dolphin football games. After telling him I was a great Dolphin fan, I called the shepherd over and said, "Let me introduce you to my dog Shula."

"Boy," he said, "Wait until I tell Don he has a dog named after him out in the Ten Thousand Islands."

`Which he apparently did because a few weeks later I got Shula's picture in the mail.

But that is not the end of the story.

All along I was puzzled about one small item. The dog Shula was a female. I couldn't for the life of me figure out why anyone would have named a female dog after Don Shula except, maybe, a member of the Baltimore Colts. Anyway, I kept harrying the thing until I remembered that the dog had previously been owned by a Spanish family. Possibly "Shula" had some different meaning in Spanish. Not long after a teacher of Spanish visited here with a group and I asked her about it. She thought a moment and said, "No, Shula doesn't mean anything in Spanish, but Chula does. It means 'pretty girl.'"

The solution. The dog was appropriately named after all and only through our ignorant habit of Americanizing foreign words did it end up Shula. I shouldn't complain; I got Don's autographed picture anyway.

This next story tells how I happened to appear on a television show.

It all began with the arrival one day of a pleasant-spoken man accompanied by a very attractive young woman. The visit started off in the usual manner with me describing things about the Indian mound, showing them my tray of artifacts and answering the usual questions about life on an island. But before long, as they settled into my easy chairs, I became aware that they were boring a bit deeper than most people do into things … my personal life in particular.

This was not especially disconcerting to me. My life is pretty much of an open book for anyone interested. I make no effort to conceal the fact that I'm an alcoholic and that is the primary reason I'm living out here. Nevertheless, I felt that there was some ulterior motive in their questioning. I began to imagine a bunch of things … maybe they were from Internal Revenue trying to find out why I hadn't been submitting income tax returns for some years although I was certain that with no fixed income whatsoever, I was relieved of that yearly chore. Then, I wondered if I had somehow inadvertently broken the law at some time or other and these were detectives.

After a bit my curiosity got the better of me and I flat out asked them how come they were so curious about the details of my life. They laughed then and told me that they represented a private film company that was making a series of documentary films for television on American waterways. One of these films was to be called "Gateway to the Everglades" and covered the Ten Thousand Island area as being not only picturesque but also of great ecological importance. They had heard that there was a hermit living out here and they had come to see if said hermit might be interesting enough to include in the filming.

"After all," the man said, "you might have been an illiterate moron or so anti-social that we could never learn enough about you to make it interesting. But, he assured me, "We are happy to find that you don't fit either category."

They asked me if I would be willing to be filmed and interview for their enterprise. When I assured them I could be delighted, they told me that my final interview would be with no less a celebrity than James Franciscus of television and movie fame.

Before that, however, a TV crew of eight or nine guys came out one day with all their sound and camera equipment and spent six hours filming every aspect of my life that we could think of from getting up in the morning and fixing breakfast to reading at night by lamplight … and everything in between … hiking the trails, digging for artifacts, fishing off the dock, painting and playing my accordion.

It was just like in the movies about making movies. There was a guy with the black and white striped clapper board with the "Scene two - take three" routine and the "action – camera" cries and more cries of "cut!" and, "Let's do that over again and this time move a little to your left." Believe me, when that day was done I was plumb wore out and I suddenly knew that there was a great deal more involved in making movies than looking glamorous.

Three or four weeks later several charter boats converged on my dock and when I went down to greet the visitors I was introduced to James Franciscus and Julius Boris and several other people of importance … director, producer, secretaries, and I don't know who-all.

While this was going on, our attention was drawn to a low flying plane circling overhead and I was told that that was part of the crew taking aerial movies of the proceedings.

The director then explained how the meeting with Franciscus should take place … how I should hear his boat approaching and walk out on the dock to grab a line and help him tie up and then greet him with a handshake and all. So the boats all pulled away and his boat came in first, following the directions as the plane filmed it all from overhead and cameras in a following boat got it at sea level.

After this we walked up to the house together and inside he looked over my paintings and the interview began with him asking me pretty much the same questions I had been asked before about my reasons for living out here in the boonies; how I managed without refrigeration; what I did with myself all day; and how I felt about living alone.

When it was all over and the whole gang began to drift back toward the boats, the director took me aside and handed me a hundred dollar bill for my cooperation in the venture. Which was really exciting because it was the first time in my life I had ever held a hundred-dollar bill in my hands.

Aside from the fun of the thing and the bonus, I had the exaggerated idea that once the film was shown on TV, I would be swamped with visitors coming out of curiosity to see the hermit who had appeared with James Franciscus. It didn't work out that way. During following year I had visitors from various parts of the country who casually mentioned that they had seen me on TV but I don't believe any of them came as a result of the showing.

I forgot to mention that in the group with Ted Williams was another celebrity possibly as well known as the ball player. This was Don MacNeil of radio and television fame ... something to do with a breakfast club. My apologies to Mr. MacNeil for not being familiar with his program! I'm afraid I must truly have missed something there because whenever I point out his signature in my guest book people smile and say, "Yeah. Don MacNeil. Yeah." Maybe that doesn't sound like much of an accolade, but the smiles and tone of voice carry more weight than words.

Anyway, that covers the celebrities that I know about, by which I mean that there may have been other people of note visiting here that I didn't recognize and who for reasons of their own didn't say who they were.

This idea is not as far-fetched as it sounds. You see, most of my visitors are out in this area fishing or sightseeing or picnicking or something and are invariably dressed in old clothes or sport clothes or practically no clothes so there is nothing about their appearance to indicate what station they may hold in life. I've been embarrassed a couple of times during the hodge-podge conversation when I've spouted some pseudo knowledge about medical mattes only to discover that I'm talking to a doctor. I've had many doctors visit here as well as lawyers, bankers, teachers, artists, writers, and businessmen ... even one atomic scientist. Rich and poor they come ... in all types of craft from prams to seagoing yachts.

Of course I get and occasional kook, too. The one I am going to tell you about can't be offended if he finds himself so categorized because I hasten to say that to this day I am not sure whether he was truly a nut or if he was simply a clever actor pulling my leg. At any rate he said he was a professional treasure hunter. This led to a brisk conversation because among other things this is a treasure-hunting country. After regaling me with many of his experiences, I told him about the unfruitful attempts of so many people to find treasure on Panther Key around the pirate Gomez's old home site.

He said, "I can tell you in a minute whether there is treasure there or not if you have a map or chart of the place."

As I got out my chart I wondered what branch of the occult I was about to see demonstrated. It had to be something like that I figured. I spread it out on the table put my finger on Panther Key. He made some remark and fumbled around in his shirt pocket, finally bringing forth a small glass ball attached to a string about a foot long. Resting his elbow on the table he suspended the little pall from finger and thumb so that it hung directly over Gomez Point on the map. We watched in silence for the best part of a minute. Nothing happened.

Finally he said, "Nossir. 'there's nary a bit of treasure there."

"How can you tell?" I asked him.

"You didn't see the crystal ball moving any didja?"

"You mean if it moves it indicates buried treasure?"

"You got it."

Try it on Hog Key," I suggested. "Ole Gomez used to tell people he had a cache of emeralds buried there."

I showed him where Hog Key was and he suspended the ball over it. Very quickly the little ball began to wing slowly back and forth. This time I was watching his hand and fingers instead of the ball but I swear I could not detect any muscular movement of any kind.

"There y'are," he said. "There's something buried on that island alright."

I trust I displayed the proper amount of amazement and said, "I expect you'll be the lucky one to go and find them."

"Oh no," he replied, "I'm only interested in sunken Spanish ships with their cargos of gold."

He caressed his little crystal then and said, "This really has the power. Why, I can suspend it over a photograph of a person and tell you whether he is alive or dead."

"I'd like to see that," I said as I shuffled through my box of photos and found one of my predecessor, Foster. As I put it in front of him I asked him if he recognized the man.

"Not likely," he said. "I've never been down in these parts before."

Again he suspended the magic ball over the photo of Foster and again it didn't move a hair.

"He's dead, I reckon."

I admitted that he was.

As I say, he could have been putting on a superb act for the benefit of a naïve hermit. But then, I think I had done a fair job myself in pretending to be taken in by it all.

Most people come and visit with me for a while and go. If they notice the cobwebs in the corners or the mud dauber's nests on the ceiling or the dirt on the floor, they are kind enough to say nothing about it. But recently, a wealthy couple was exposed a little more to the realities of my hermit life.

Just about dusk a while back I heard a sound the like of which I had never heard before. Indescribable! But to give you a hint of what it was like I might compare it to the squawk of a heron only ten times louder. Digger set up a frenzied barking and I'll admit I felt a shiver of apprehension. Nevertheless, I clapped on my hat and headed down to the dock wondering all the while what I would find capable of making such a horrible noise. What I found was a sporty fishing boat tied up to Nel's house-just across the channel. I yelled,

"Are ... You ... In ... Trouble?"

Someone yelled back, "Yes!"

I jumped into my boat after sliding it into the water and putted over to see. The man and woman there told me their motor had quit a mile or more up the channel and they had poled and paddled their way down that far before giving out. They had approached the houseboat from a different direction so that I didn't see them go by ... nor hear them, obviously. The noise I had heard was their emergency horn, which had not been used in a long time, if ever, and had become rusty or corroded and instead of giving forth a high piercing shriek had simply blatted like a dying animal.

I offered to let them use my boat to get back to town but advised against it because it was so nearly dark and they admitted that they weren't too sure of finding their way. As an alternative I invited them to stay the night with me and see about their boat in the morning. Which they did.

They were a very pleasant middle-aged couple, dressed in the usual sport outfits and it was only after I had fed them some spam and baked beans and given them all the water they needed to drink after their exertions in the hot sun that we got to talking about general things.

I asked the man what business or profession he was in and he mentioned several manufacturing enterprises, which didn't mean much to me until his wife asked if I was familiar with Argo starch, and one or two other name brand items.

"That's him," she said. I don't recall just where he fit in the corporation hierarchy but I realized that they were undoubtedly very wealthy people. I was at once thankful that I could make up the two spare beds with clean sheets.

They assured me in the morning that they had slept well though I was awakened once or twice by rats waltzing in the attic and I tried to imagine what it must have been like for people used to only the most luxurious living accommodations to find themselves in my primitive digs.

They were very appreciative, however, knowing that otherwise they'd have spent a miserable night in an open boat without food or water or sleeping pads.

Their motor problem was easily solved. They had ruptured the gas line and I loaned them my gas tank and hose to get home with. The next day they brought my tank back filled and a huge bag of fresh fruit and goodies. It all worked out very well, but I'll bet they have gotten a lot of mileage out of telling their friends about the night they spent on Dismal Key.

Quite in contrast to the wealthy couple: I was recently visited by a man and his wife who arrived in a somewhat weather-beaten, but sturdy ketch. (I would have said sailboat, but it did have three masts and lots of rigging so I asked if it was a schooner and got a long involved explanation of the difference between a schooner and a ketch.) They were of indeterminate age but I would guess close to my own. After the usual visit and exchange of information about ourselves they invited me aboard for a turkey dinner. But, it's not often one gets a turkey dinner like that one. They had raised the turkey. They had grown the vegetables and served homemade bread with honey from their own hives. They had pickled eggs from their own hens and fresh cucumbers from their garden. The meal was prepared on a wood-burning stove of ancient vintage and the boat was lighted with kerosene lamps. In short, they told me they were practically self sufficient on their little farm. We didn't get down to dollars and cents but I got the impression that it may cost them less to live than it does me, as primitively as I live.

I couldn't help but wonder which of the two couples was better off … the one with lots of money or the one with little. Both couples were healthy and happy and friendly. There is not question, of course, as to which couple would have the edge in the event of a national disaster.

Chapter 16

A Few More Beastie Stories

Somewhere along the line in this rambling narrative I believe I mentioned that I have only been faced with real danger a couple of times in all my years here. The interesting thing is that in both cases the danger had passed before I was actually aware of it. In the first instance the shark had already rammed out boat clean out of the water and was streaking away before I saw it. In the second situation the rattlesnake that I had come so close to putting my knee on was peacefully crawling away from me before I saw it.

Snakes

The reason my knee was involved, rather than a foot or a hand, was that I was picking key limes, not off the tree, but off the ground on my hands and knees. You give the tree a healthy shake, the limes fall to the ground and you gather them up much easier than getting your hands scratched up by the thorns trying to pick them directly from the branches. My attention then was on the little yellow limes scattered around and not where I was crawling. So it was only my great good fortune, by a miracle, by a favorable horoscope, by the grace of God, or the intercession of some patron saint (choose one), that I didn't put my knee on the rattler which I am sure would have retaliated by a swift strike somewhere on my thigh which would not have been a good place to be bitten. As it was, I detected a movement in my peripheral vision area and turning to look saw the snake not three feet away, making his unhurried and insolent progress to wherever he was going. At that point, of course, the danger was over. But my body responses were in good order. My heart pounded and my muscles stiffened as the adrenalin did its work. Then I began to shake and eventually I was able to get up and find my machete. The snake was now aware of danger and crawled under a sprawling cactus plant where I couldn't get to it. So I took what limes I already had in my bucket and left the field to Mr. Rattler.

Ecologist of the world must forgive me when I say that I have killed at least a dozen rattlesnakes on Dismal Key. It's not that I don't appreciate the fact that they contribute to nature's balance by eating rats and other small vermin. But I have to consider that if, through my carelessness or just plain bad luck I am bitten by one I would have to make my way out of the woods and down to my boat (the first tenet in snake-bite first aid is to keep the victim from moving) then eight miles by boat to the nearest point of civilization, and then thirty-six miles to the nearest hospital. That, in my way of thinking, is far from the optimum conditions for survival. Consequently, I always go into the woods armed with a long, stout club and I figure that each one that I kill is one less to worry about. Not only for myself, but or my dog, who so far hasn't demonstrated much good sense about them. Twice now, Digger has run right over a snake, apparently not even seeing it, and once he decided to sniff at the big one until it rattled at him and he pulled his nose back a few feet.

I don't know whether all the assorted information about rattlesnakes that has come my way from books and knowledgeable people is in error or whether the Dismal Key snakes have just never learned what they are supposed to do. But of all the ones I have killed or encountered, only two bothered to rattle. You can't go blithely striding around this island secure in the idea that they always give you warning. It just ain't so. Further, they are supposed to hurry away and hide. This may be partly true. Perhaps for every snake I've seen, ten have managed to get out of sight at my approach. The one I have seen, with one or two exceptions, have simply frozen in position, which is not good because if you don't happen to see them in time you are in trouble. Their protective coloring is superb in a bed of dry leaves.

One of the instances in which a rattler was kind enough to rattle supports my contention that in some ways women are more pragmatic than men. One evening a familiar boat came to the dock and I went on down to greet my friends. The only thing that differentiates this part of the story from other countless greetings of boats at the dock was that it was getting on for dark. After the usual tyings-up and unloading of much beer, we started back up the path toward the house with the boat owner in the lead. Between the time of my going down and our all coming back, a fat ole rattler had elected to cross the path. He or it was understandably shaken at the approach of a beer-laden caravan, so he coiled and gave off a fine, resounding rattle, which had the effect of freezing all of us in our tracks. The guy in the lead had a pistol in a holster, which he whipped out and let the snake have a .38 slug in the coils. This removed any danger of its striking, but in no way killed it. So the good man took careful aim and fired again ... trying for the head. He missed ... and missed again. His shots were so close that the air concussion from the passing slug whipped the snake's head first one way and then the other. By now we are all gathered around in fascination at the so close but not close enough marksmanship. Until the guy's wife, who apparently had no faith in the serpent's inability to be dangerous, went off and came back with a cement block which she calmly dropped on ole rattler's bean, making a clean *finis*. As I say, a woman will often hit it right on the head, first crack.

Well, rattlesnakes are a part of my life on Dismal Key, but I regret it. As it is I have to devote most of my attention to the ground ahead of and around me when I am walking my trails when I would rather be looking for birds, or tree snails, or new and different plants.

Rats

Snakes in general don't bother me. There are rats in this old house ... up in the attic mostly. I put out rat poison and get rid of them for a month or two until a new brood moves in. Because the rats are more often here than not here; I occasionally find a rat snake in the house which bothers me not at all. There is one corner of my kitchen up over the sink where the rats usually build a nest. I can see them, but can't get at them due to the way the area is boarded up. So they are safe … usually. Every now and then I'll hear a furious squeaking and when I peek in the cracks I'll see a big ole rate snake hugging a rat to death. They are constrictors, as I suppose you know.

Once I was quite amused at the behavior of the rats. There was a new family coming along in that corner. I heard the squeaks and saw the snake, but aside from the baby rat it was demolishing, the corner was deserted. Shortly, thereafter I heard a commotion in the attic. I think the mother rat had managed to get the rest of her offspring to safety and she was giving them a stiff lecture. Of all the chittering and squeaking! Of course I don't know that to be a fact, I'm just guessing, but it certainly seemed logical that she would use the object lesson to good advantage and enforce it with sound motherly advice about taking to the rafters at the first slither of a rat snake.

Rats are intelligent buggers anyway. As I say, I put out rat poison regularly and usually it's effective. Not always. Sometimes only the young or ignorant ones will eat it. Often it will go untouched altogether. Once I mixed it with granola and later found the granola gone and the poison untouched. Fortunately, the rats don't do much damage. They leave their little calling cards all over and sometimes get into a bag of dry dog food. Mostly, the problem is with the noise they make at night. They tromp around in the attic as if having a ball game and in the kitchen will knock dishes off the table, cast off skillets, and get ole Digger in a sweat chasing them around and barking at the ceiling. Once in awhile he'll even catch one.

Why don't I keep a cat? Simple. I hate cats.

Possum

One night, or rather about three one morning, I was awakened by what sounded like a dogfight in the kitchen. I grabbed my light and fell out of bed to investigate. There was Digger, growling and snarling as he tackled what appeared to be the biggest rat I had ever seen. In the blur of action, all I could really see and then only sporadically, was a rat-like tail at least a foot long. I remember thinking, "It can't be … there just aren't any rats that big!" It wasn't. In no time Digger had gotten a fresh purchase on the critter's neck and thrashed it to a standstill. It was a possum. Which in itself was very interesting because I had never seen a possum before on these islands.

Once Digger had it whipped or so he thought, he dragged it into the living room onto my one and only rug and looked up to me for praise he was sure he'd get. I told him what a fine, fearless dog he was, and giving the ugly looking possum a final look, went back to bed. I had just about conked off again when the growling and barking started all over again. I got a broom and shoved the possum out where he could go at it again. In short order it appeared that the possum was dead. I even whacked it a couple of times with the broom handle to make sure.

Instead of going back to bed, though, I sat down to watch. Yup. In a few minutes it started to raise its head and then tried to get to its feet despite being a bloody mess and fatally wounded. That time I got a wrecking bar and made sure it was dead. So now I knew where the phrase, "playing possum" originated from and I also learned that this generally inoffensive creatures has a most tenacious hold on life. I'll say nothing about my bloody carpet.

Since then I have seen one other possums on Dismal … one Digger that had treed. That one, I am happy to say, got away with no more than a fright. But now when people asked me what kinds of animals live here, I can add possums to the list.

Some animal or animals must have contributed to one of the mysteries of Dismal Key. Down the hill from the house and off to one side is an area that for no good reason I have dubbed "the lower forty." It is a relatively flat area covering several acres and is divided into five equal sections by what I can only assume to be the remains of Calusa Indian Canals. These ditches, fairly well grown now with mangroves and buttonwoods are so straight, so parallel and so evenly spaced that they must have had human origin. Anyway, I have a sort of trail out across this area and on one of my daily walks I noticed a gumbo-limbo tree with a sizeable hole in the trunk about eight feet from the ground. On closer inspection I noted scratch marks in the bark below it and assumed that it was probably a sanctuary for a family of 'coons. The hole seemed too big for rats. The tree was there after known as the "'coon tree." I used it as a landmark to cut a transverse trail between the lower forty and the middle cistern. A year passed without giving more than a cursory glance at the 'coon hole before I noticed that it was closing up. Sure enough, the tree was healing this wound in its trunk by growing scar tissue. For some months I watched this process until the hole was almost closed. Then, it was suddenly opened again. Fairly sizeable chips of fresh wood were on the ground at the foot of the tree and the hole had clearly identifiable tooth marks.

I figured that a new family of coons had found the hole, decided to utilize it and were enlarging the entrance. However, I had some guests with me one time and told them about the strange goings on with this hole. One of the guys got a long twig and began poking it around in the hole … hoping to run the coons out or something. Anyway, nothing happened and after poking a little more, he said, "That's funny … the hole doesn't go anywhere."

"What do you mean?" I asked him.

"Why look here," he said as he rammed his twig into the hole again and then his hand. "The hole doesn't go up or down at all. What you see is what there is."

I verified it. So there you are. Did coons or rats or some other critter live in the hole before? Was the tree hollow then? If the tree was never hollow why did some animal go to the trouble of opening the hole again? Your guess may be better than mine. And yes, the tree has started to scab the hole over again.

Among the smaller creatures on the island, some are very colorful. Some fantastic. A large, brilliant yellow and black spider is common and a nuisance since it (she) always insists on hanging a web directly across any path I cut.

Then, there are hundreds of the little Anoles generally called Chameleons, that change color from a bright emerald green to dull brown and when courting puff out a ball of skin under their chins in flashy orange and red.

In the fantastic department are a couple of tiny spiders that don't resemble spiders at all. One, I believe is called the crab spider because it has a square-body. Another I have not been able to identify has a body shaped like the fins of a rocket ship. I presume they are both spiders since they spin webs to catch tiny flies and gnats.

A frequent guest in my house is the five-lined skink, a small blue and brown lizard. They come for flies and cockroaches, so I never bother them. Digger loves to chase them though.

A hermit isn't supposed to be much of a housekeeper, but when I first noticed hundreds of tiny, compact spider's nests about the size of a quarter proliferating on my ceiling, I figured it was too much and got a whisk broom to brush them down. On closer inspection, however, I discovered that the nests were loaded with sand fly carcasses so I let them stay. Anything that can reduce the sand fly population is a real friend of mine.

Scorpions

I almost wound this chapter up without mentioning the scorpions. There are scorpions everywhere, inside and out. They love to crawl between books and papers and get into cardboard boxes and sometimes shoes. Outside, they can be found under loose bark on dead trees, or in and around any dead wood; also under cans or boxes. However, these Dismal Key scorpions are a small, brown variety that is neither dangerous nor very aggressive. Oh, they'll sting you fast enough if you give 'em a chance, but the sting is no worse than an average bee sting, painful for a few minutes only. They are slow moving critters, so that now I know where to expect to find them, I simply shake things out, or lift boxes gingerly. Sometimes I stomp on them, but more often than not I let them alone. I'm not sure what they prey on, but whatever it is may be more of a nuisance than the scorpions themselves.

The only slight problem I ever had with them was back when I had Barbie. If she saw one crawling across the floor, she would catch it in her teeth and snap it into the air, which would be O.K. with me if she watched where she was snapping them-to. Once or twice the damn things landed in my lap causing me to do a bit of snapping too.

Once, I saw a scorpion crawling very slowly up a wall. It seemed to be a new or different variety with a variegated pattern on its back. I poked it into a glass jar only to see the variegations peel off and become baby scorpions. Like one or two other strange creatures in the world, scorpion mothers carry their young around on their backs.

Al Seely and Willie on Dismal Key, June 1972 (Courtesy of Bob Steele)

Chapter 17

Pseudo-profundities

This is the second time I have come to grips with the sticky problem of bringing this narrative to a close. The first time I got bogged down in lengthy and sordid reflections about the approaching end of my life. This type of conclusion would have been all right if it contained some profound message derived from my solitary and close-to-nature existence. If, let us say, I could tell how I had achieved vast inner peace from being in tune with the wind and tides or flow and ebb of seasons in my hermitage. But, whenever I get occasional feelings of tranquility, they usually turn out, on closer analysis, to be a type of somnolence or coma induced by boredom, which is mostly what has resulted from the sameness of my days, my diet, and my activities. At least, if I can't expound on the great mystique of solitude, I can admit that it's nice not to be under the usual pressures of civilization.

One of the things I did achieve out here was the ability to turn my head off. This was a necessary thing because with so much time to think I would have been driven up the nearest gumbo-limbo in an effort to find some deep meaning and abiding significance in my life. So, it is hardly fitting for me to make even a feeble attempt at last chapter philosophy.

Instead, I shall utilize my brain in the manner to which it has become accustomed, letting it spew out bits and pieces of ideas, comments and other trivia …things that slide into and out of my mind from time to time.

~

For instance, I've been hearing a lot on the radio about women's liberation. Now that's a big subject … issue … or whatever. In order to pass any judgment on the matter, I'd have to turn my head back on. But, I can comment briefly on one aspect of it, and, incidentally, anyone … any man, that is, who may be contemplating the joys of becoming a hermit, should pay attention here. As a hermit, if I want to eat, I gotta cook. If I want clean clothes and fresh sheets on my bed, I gotta do the frigging laundry. If I want people to continue to visit me, I gotta sweep the floor once in awhile and keep my house in some kind of order. All woman's work. I imagine that most men have some woman around, a wife or mother or sister or mistress, to relieve them of most of these icky chores. For most of my life I took it for granted that this was what women did. So from one male chauvinist pig to another, let me suggest that you try hermiting for awhile long enough anyway to appreciate what your women do for you day in and day out – no weekends off. I don't know if I advocate complete liberation of women from these aspects of life because then we'd have to start a men's liberation movement or something. But, I do strongly advocate that women be given a round of applause, a medal, a pat on the back, or a buss on the left nipple … some expression of appreciation for the many things they do to make our lives more comfortable.

~

Throughout these chapters I have had quite a bit to relate about animal life out here. I have constantly been intrigued with the differences between animal and human behavior some important, some not. There is one difference, however, which may be significant. Man alone, of all the animals on earth, has to use toilet paper.

~

Every now and then you hear some more about the relationship between brain size and intelligence i.e. the bigger the brain the more intelligent. There's no doubt a lot of truth in these theories, but it can't be the whole truth since if it were the lowly elephant would lead the parade. As far as I know, no elephant has even invented the wheel. Going in the opposite direction, one is often surprised at the amount of intelligence to be found in tiny brains. I am thinking now of a kind of spider that infests my house. It is sort of a "daddy-long-legs" thing and the body is not as large as a B B shot, the head smaller than the head of a pin. But, I have watched them warily stalk a small moth fluttering at the window, then with a dash, catch it, and with an exquisite ballet in space, truss it up for future dinners. I have also watched a couple of them chase each other around in real or simulated fight. This would seem to indicate an emotional response to something or other ... territory, sex, male machismo, or something. So I marvel at the strange intricacies and manifestations of intelligence and emotion in nature large and small, and wonder about it, too ... but not very long.

~

When I turn my radio on in the mornings for the news from Miami, I generally hear one or two reports from the "sky patrol." There is a guy who flies up and down and around in a helicopter, I guess, and he watches the flow of traffic. Whenever he spots a jam or backup he not only reports its location, but suggests alternate routes. A very fine service for those poor clods that have to drive into the city every day to go to work. Providing they have their car radios on and providing they listen to his advice, which is doubtful.

Obviously, being snug and smug and secure on my island, I couldn't care less about the traffic situation in greater Miami. Since I have to listen to it anyway, I have gotten into the habit of trying to imagine myself up there in the 'copter seeing the overall picture as the reporter sees it. I don't really think my imagination is capable of conjuring up the hundreds of thousands of cars speeding along the many four and six lane arteries into the city; and as many thousands going the other way to destinations in the suburbs.

Once a year or so I go over to the megalopolis for a week or two and have often found myself being driven along one of these horrors, at least that is how I see it whenever I am courageous enough to open my eyes. People who are accustomed to that kind of daily driving look askance at me when I say that it scares the bejesus out of me. But then, they have not been confined, as I have for ten years, to boat travel with a top speed of ten miles per hour and no traffic whatsoever. Zooming down a crowded freeway at fifty-five is, for me, a truly bowel-loosening experience.

Well, let them laugh at me, I say. I am justified in being petrified. I hear the sky patrol almost every day describing a bash-up here, a three-car collision there, a trailer-truck jackknifed on the highway, someone ramming a utility pole somewhere else, and the reports of police and fire units and ambulances rushing to the scenes of blood and broken glass. As I imagine myself up there in the helicopter seeing it all, I can only think: "Hot Damn! I'm not so dumb after all to come out here and live on an island where rattlesnakes are the worst-thing I have to worry about."

~

There were some campaign blurbs on the radio this morning for some local politicians seeking minor offices like city councilman or school board member and one of them had taken the privilege of improving our language. Heretofore, it had been acceptable to refer to things like community action, community spirit, and community this or that. No longer. Now it is "communitarian." Jeez!

~

Charlotte solved a problem for me recently. The problem was this: how do I cope with the countless visitors who tender good advice that I have no intention of heeding. It goes like this:

"WHY DON'T YOU-

- Install a generator so you can have a refrigerator or air conditioning, or TV.
- Build a windmill for the same purposes.
- Build a fish smoker.
- Turn a couple of hogs loose on the island to get rid of the rattlesnakes and also provide pork chops
- Build a fish trap.
- Have a goat to thin out the underbrush.
- Get automobile batteries to install a 12-volt electrical system for lights.
- Raise bees for honey.
- Plant a garden
- On and on and on …

The minute I hear those prefatory words "why don't you," my mind goes on red alert to come up with reasonable reasons why I don't want to do whatever is about to be suggested. This usually leads to a friendly argument and usually I end up seeming quite the fool.

No more. When I told Charlotte about it she, in her vast female wisdom, said: "How can they expect you to do all these things? Don't they realize that it takes time to be a hermit?" Right on! Even I didn't realize how much time it takes to be a hermit. But, now that I do, I have the perfect foil for the why-don't-you's.

~

Anyone who has fished in the Ten Thousand Island area for any length of time knows that each year it becomes more difficult to catch a decent string. People seem to think I ought to know why this is so. I don't of course, but to answer the repeated question, I have come up with the following formula: at a conservative estimate, one boat out of twenty going by here will stop for a visit. Since I average at least 600 visitors per year that means that 12,000 boats pass here each year. In the last ten years, 120,000 boats have been fishing in this area. If you then made a conservative estimate of three fish caught per boat you would see that in the last ten years they have taken 360,000 fish from these waters. Just for a guess perhaps 60,000 of these were female fish bearing eggs. I looked it up in the encyclopedia and found that a female fish can lay anywhere up to nine million eggs. But, again we'll keep it minimal and say that each of the 60,000 eggs that didn't get laid or several million fish that never got born or reached maturity. Add the millions of fish that didn't make it to begin with to the 360,000 that were summarily removed…

Well, there are probably some flaws in the calculations somewhere, but it makes you think; to say nothing of the pollution to the water from all those outboard, inboard, and inboard-outboard motors.

Going back to women's liberation for a minute, did you hear that in one town or country or somewhere they changed the wording of one of the local ordinances so that one is no longer prosecuted as a "peeping tom" but only as a "peeping person." It does alliterate anyway.

~

It's very damn seldom that I come up with a totally original idea.

If there is such a thing.

One came to me yesterday, but for accuracy's sake there is a possibility that someone in Alaska or Bangkok has already thought about it. As far as I know it is original with me as of this date.

I've been visiting Charlotte for a few days and I spotted a dress in her closet that had the most gorgeous colors. A truly beautiful fabric. And I thought, "Wouldn't that look super as a wall hanging, draped in some artistic manner to provide maximum composition without hiding the fact that it is a dress."

Now, it is prophecy time. I predict that sometime, somewhere, using garments in home décor will be *de rigueur*. It will be tough on the Salvation Army though.

From my somewhat limited knowledge of the subject I would guess that hermits don't have much use for soap. This hermit doesn't anyway. I suspect that my aversion to bathing stems from my childhood years when every Saturday night I was plonked into the old copper bathtub and scrubbed vigorously with soap and a Lysol solution so strong that my little ole balls burned for a couple of hours after each treatment. Fact.

So, when I got a snappy little advertising folder in the mail the other day devoted to the sale of soap I gave a snort and was about to pitch it in the wastebasket when it hit me that this was no ordinary soap being offered so invitingly. In fact, this was a whole spectrum of soaps each containing some special ingredient. In each case there was an explanation of why this particular soap with this particular ingredient was so beneficial to your health, happiness, and fragrance.

You probably won't believe it anymore than I did but it's fact. These various soaps contained things like seaweed, rainwater, honey, avocado, birch leaves, tomatoes, carrots, lettuce, beeswax, mink oil (dig that one), ginger ale, milk, sulphur (ugh) buttermilk, eggs, and coal tar. In addition there was non-soap and soapless soap, whatever the difference there might be.

Wow! It almost made me think I'd better stop being a hermit so I could take advantage of all these wonderful cleaning and deodorizing agents. But then I thought what the hell! I could probably mush up some ordinary soap and add a few ingredients more suited to a hermit-such as fish scales, (fine abrasive action), or boiled tree snails, or coon droppings.

I probably won't bother though because I am afraid Digger might get very upset if I didn't exude my usual ripe, *hermity* odor.

~

Among all the professional men and women who have visited me I can't recall a single psychiatrist or psychologist. There may have been one or two who kept their specialty secret in order to make a quick study of the kooky hermit without my knowing it. But, someday I hope one comes along and I do know about it so I can ask about the significance of green. That's right ... the color green. Perhaps significance is not the word. Perhaps what I mean is the effect of the color green on me ... on my psyche, or emotions, spirit, or whatever. How I feel anyway.

Because, you see, I am surrounded by green. All the shades of green there are, I think. Through my rather small windows I can get but a glimpse of the sky here and there. And looking down the vista in front of the house I can see only a small patch of blue-brown-gray water. Everything else is green; north, south, east and west, trees, shrubs, leaves, lawn, weeds and seeds: ... green ... green.

There was a time some years ago when I was starved for the green of a tree or plant. When we bought our house in Hollywood it was in a new development and aside from a couple of scrawny shrubs at the front door, the entire lot was nothing but sand. As was true of all the houses up and down the street and in the street behind us. We'd have been just as comfortable in the Sahara Desert. At least the monotony there is relieved by a pyramid or two. So for years we nurtured anything that would grow ... just for the comfort of having green things close at hand.

So, why am I complaining now that I am at the other extreme, you might say, and am living in a veritable jungle of green growing things. But that's just it, I think. There is too damn much green. I try to console myself with the thought that every leaf is giving off oxygen and with no smog nearby I must have the best air in Florida. That works for a while. Then, I often paint landscapes and I am grateful to have all the shades of green at hand to go by. But every so often when I am feeling a bit green around the gills, as they say, and I am opening a can of Jolly Green Giant peas, I can barely restrain myself from gong into a fit of the screaming greenies.

It would be just my luck to have the psychologist, if one ever comes, tell me that green has a most soothing effect on one's mind and soul. If that is true, of course, I'm in a helluva shape.

~

If I were to turn my head back on, or even if I only banged on it a few times I could probably go on with this kind of trivia until we were both bored out of our skulls. Enough is enough.

FINIS

Last sketch

Epilog
Mark Cowell

YALONDA M. JAMES/STAFF
Mark Cowell, director of the Charleston County Department of Alcohol and Other Drug Services, in his office at the Charleston Center.

October 11, 2004

Betsy,

I'll be happy to add my own thoughts as they come to me … and you can use whatever I send in paraphrase, direct quote, whatever. I should add, however, that it has been a long time and memory is selective and not always accurate. But I'll do my best.

The "palace" on Dismal Key was certainly an uptown move for my Dad. There was a hierarchy of *hermitdom* in the Ten Thousand Islands and Dad made his way up the ladder over time. To give you a sense of comparison from the Dismal Key, I am sending you two photographs I found of his initial digs on Brush Key. I apologize for the quality but I recently upgraded my computer and don't have the disks to install the scanner so I had to make a copy of the snapshots using a digital camera. I have a few more coming next week - one of his places on Panther Key. His move up the ladder of hermit success went from Brush Key where he only had a tent, to Panther Key where he had one room on stilts, to Dismal, where your account starts.

When he first moved to the blue tent on Brush Key, I don't think anyone, including himself, thought he'd last very long. At that time, he was a late stage chronic alcoholic - and I say that with great love and affection because I have shared the same disease and the same genes as my old man. But my own legacy of alcoholism was just getting off the ground at college parties at Northeastern University when his was grinding toward a potentially tragic finish. He had been diagnosed with cirrhosis of the liver and given only a short time to live. He was unemployable, on welfare, and dying of alcoholism. His decision to leave society and become a hermit was not done out of a sense of adventure but out of a combination of despair and grabbing for straws. I'm not sure that he didn't intend to just go out there and die. I expected that he'd stay for a week, give up, and try something else.

But after a couple of months, it began to look like he was on to something. I went down on spring break to visit him. I had not seen him a lot in my life. After my mother, his first wife, Jean, died when I was seven, he was unable to raise me because of the alcoholism. After he remarried, I spent a few miserable months living with him and Charlotte before he wrote my grandparents (Jean's parents - Joseph and Helen Cowell) and they agreed to raise me. Helen was a violinist and Joseph was an artist and sculptor (he designed and did the woodcarving and painting of the Children's Chapel at the National Cathedral in Washington, DC). My grandparents legally adopted me, by the way, with his blessing, which is why my name is Mark Andover Seely Cowell. It was the constant insistence of Helen (who I called Gramzee) that I stay in touch with him, writing him letters, or I might have lost touch with him entirely.

On my visit to Brush Key I mostly remember being afraid of rattlesnakes and how he and I cut branches from mangrove trees and constructed a makeshift bed for me in the tent, so I would be raised off the ground. We worked all afternoon of the first day trying to tie these tangles of mangrove roots and vines together. That first night I tossed and turned on the most uncomfortable bed I've ever tried to sleep in. The next night I decided what he had already known, that a potential rattlesnake in my sleeping bag was far preferable to a bed frame made from mangrove trees.

At that time, he was still trying to augment his monthly disability check by selling starfish to retailers in shells and crafts. We spent endless boring hours walking the meager Brush Key beach and collecting starfish, which we laid out in the sun to dry all around the campsite. The odor from hundreds of starfish cooking in the sun quickly dispensed any stereotypes of fresh ocean breezes in a tropical paradise.

At that point, he was still trying to follow his intention to live as much as possible off the land. Later when he discovered it was more profitable to sell his paintings to the rich folks who chartered fishing excursions, he stopped the starfish idea and also lived more from canned goods he bought in Goodland. But on that first visit, I remember trying to pick the stickers out of cactus buds and make a kind of sour jelly and trying to figure out a way of seasoning some species of boiled sea oat or grass so that it could be swallowed without gagging. When it came time for me to leave the island, he took me back in his small motorboat. After our goodbyes and after he had motored out of sight, I went straight to some little fishing camp store in Goodland and ordered a cheeseburger and a cold beer. To this day, I remember it as the best meal I've ever eaten.

~

During his stint in Florida, he began multiple attempts to stop sober and quit drinking. He went through numerous hospitalizations and detoxifications. He would go to A.A. for awhile and then relapse. In fact, on one of my visits, when I was 13 or so, he took me along to an A.A. meeting and I remember being bored and mostly watching a cockroach crawling on the floor between people's legs. When I was 16, he started going to A.A. again, trying to make it again, and had put enough time together so it looked like it might work. He even got together with some other recovering alcoholics and started a halfway house. (Early in recovery, we sometimes want to save the world!).

He invited me down so during a summer vacation from high school, I drove a rattley Triumph sedan down there. I am forbidden by Karen to tell this story to my 16-year-old son who is only allowed to drive around town during the day, but my grandparents were extremely laissez faire in my upbringing. They were Bohemian-type artist/musicians from the 1920's (an earlier generation version of Hippies) and let me drive by myself from Massachusetts to Florida when I was just 16. The first few days went well. I stayed in the halfway house he managed. Then about a week into the trip I came back from flirting with girls on the beach and found him drunk. Shocked and discouraged, I left the house and stayed with Charlotte. The next day she went to work and I was asleep when he broke in the front door. He was looking for money. He was drunk. He went into her bedroom and started to drink some of her perfume. If I knew then some of the things I would drink in my own later stages of alcoholism, I wouldn't have been so shocked, but I jumped on him to try and take it away from him and we crashed around the room, breaking Charlotte's closet door with the back of my head when he fell back against me. He ran out shortly afterwards. I was going to stick around and help out but then Charlotte came home, learned about what had happened, and drove over to the halfway house to give him some money. I drove back to Massachusetts. That was probably the low point. And I had very little to do with him for the next few years until he moved to Brush Key.

I promised to tell you this story.

The highpoint came many years later and about five years before his death. He corresponded by mail from Massachusetts to Florida, it took the mail about 3 to 4 days to get there. He had finally had to move off of Dismal Key and go back to Goodland. His eyesight was getting poor and he was having trouble seeing snakes in time and had a couple of frighteningly close calls with rattlers. He moved back to Goodland to live in an abandoned house trailer.

During his time in the islands, he never stopped drinking, incidentally. There were often long periods of time in between when he could get alcohol because of isolation and money. But whenever he went into Goodland to get his disability check and provisions, he would also get enough alcohol so he could put on a good bender and would then wake up somewhere, lost, in the bottom of his small boat. Also, fishing boat captains would bring out their charters and they would often leave him a bottle or two. But the hard work and time in between binges kept him in fairly good physical shape.

Anyhow, he had gone back to Goodland where alcohol was more available and was going downhill again. By that time, I had gotten sober, was going steadily to A.A. and had seven years of sobriety under by belt. Actually, I had seven years of "being dry," it is possible to go to meetings but not actually put any real effort into the 12-Steps of A.A. and achieve what is called "white knuckle sobriety." In essence, all I had achieved was to go from being a drunken asshole to being a sober asshole. But around my seventh year, I finally got serious about the program and started working the Steps very hard. I don't know how much you know about the Steps but the 8th Step is "Made a list of all persons we had harmed, and became willing to make amends to them all," and the 9th Step is "Made direct amends to such people wherever possible, except when to do so would injure them or others." I had made lots of tough amends to people but never thought I owed one to him since he had, after all, abandoned me, and I had never hurt him. But one day I realized that for the past several years I had been treating him condescendingly. I knew by then that he had a disease, the same one I did. But I justified myself that I was sober and successful and he was still a drunk. My letters preached to him. Realizing what I had been doing I knew I owed him amends and I sat down and wrote a long letter of amends for my behavior. I mailed it.

Two days later (remembering that it took 3 days for the mail to get from one place to the other) I received a letter from him. Without my knowing it, he had started going to A.A. again, but this time for the last time, and he was working the Steps, and it was his amends letter to me. They had crossed in the mail! Looking at the dates, we later realized that had to be more than simple coincidence, we had been sitting and writing amends letters to each other at the exact same time without knowing it! If there was ever an experience that strengthened my belief in God, that was it. He never drank again. A few years later, I married Karen, also recovering, who I met at an A.A. Convention in Georgia. She and I visited him in Goodland and went to an A.A. meeting with him. That was probably the high point.

I guess that is enough for today. I hope you don't mind endless ramblings.

~

Actually, I can't remember for sure whether this was Digger or not. He had two dogs, I believe while he was there. I can't remember whether Digger was the first or the second. I think the first. So this would be Digger. He got his second dog after his first disappeared. He was not sure whether Digger (we'll assume it was the first) disappeared due to alligator, panther, or turtle poacher. He had a run in with turtle poachers while on Brush Key. When he first was there, he reported in a letter to me that after the first few days he began having auditory hallucinations because it was dead silent except for lapping surf at night and without the background noise of traffic, air conditioners, etc., that we take for granted, he began to think he heard traffic. The first time he heard loggerheads coming ashore in the middle of the night, he thought it was a bulldozer! He heard and sometimes saw turtle poachers and was always angry and sad when he found the slaughtered remains of these regal creatures in the morning. I remember on Panther Key he had a huge turtle skull perched on the top of the stair railing. One night he got angry at the turtle poachers and approached them with a bow and arrow he kept but never used. When they saw him they pulled guns and he ran into the night as gunfire broke out although he never knew whether they were shooting at him, his dog, the turtle on just into the air.

152

I can give you his background...

He was born in Athol, Massachusetts of a strictly religious mother and a father who spent most of his time in the garage tinkering and Dad and I both hypothesized drinking but no real evidence for that. Dad went, I believe, to a seminary school in Boston for awhile, then into the army. I don't think he ever saw action in the army although he learned to drink there. I don't remember the machinist part of his pretty itinerant resume. He worked lots of odd jobs - I remember he managed a movie theater for awhile. He played violin, accordion, and bass fiddle. During one of the brief times I lived with him in Maryland (where we all lived around the time my mother died) he was playing bass fiddle in a country music band, playing in roadside bars. I think he was pretty well read but I don't know much about his tastes. I know that while in the Ten Thousand Islands he liked mysteries. When my wife, Karen and I went down for his funeral and to clean out his effects, Karen took back a complete collection of paperback Agatha Christie novels. And he read a lot of science fiction as well. He played chess and next week I'll send a picture I took of us (tripod, delayed shutter) playing chess by lantern light in the shack on Panther. I'll add two more pictures I have today of him including one where he is wearing a t-shirt I had made and sent him for Christmas that reads Dismal Key Softball Team.

Your friend Mark.

Letter from Charlotte Seely

October 19, 2004
Dear Betsy,

Thank you for your letter with its enclosed copies of your column, Days Gone By. Reading your quotations from Al's journal reminds me of the disarming candor and charm of his writing. I remember the things we shared, our letters, the visits back and forth between the island and Hollywood. Take the top off the box, and everything inside is there intact, fresh, vibrant.

I'm glad that you have permission to publish the journal in its entirety. Thank you for sending the Veteran's Marker photograph. I visited the Pioneer Cemetery in 1996 and saw that the last name was incorrectly spelled; I think that has been corrected.

My house came through the hurricanes with out damage. I was without electricity for seven days as a result of Hurricane Jeanne. The trucks the power line crew drove were from Houston, Texas. I showed one of the crew a Carambolla from my tree, to which foreign object they had little reaction beyond common courtesy!

Thank you again for your kindness in sending me your two columns. It was thoughtful of you to remember.

Sincerely
Charlotte R. Seely

P.S. If this typeface looks familiar, it may be the one you recognize from Al's journal. We had two Royal portables, one elite (this one), the other pica, this one. We traded them back and forth as necessary. I recently had both refurbished, and use them sometimes, just for old times sake.

The following letter from Charlotte Seely shows the actual typewriter font used by Al in his manuscript:

810 N.W. 70th Avenue
Hollywood, FL , 33024
February 15, 2005

Dear Betsy,

Your letter was a nice surprise. I especially appreciate your comparison of Al to O. Henry. I always enjoyed his easy, flowing style. Some writers who present a seemingly effortless style say they labor over it. I think it came easily to him.

I like what you said about your journey of getting to know Al as you typed his journal into your computer. Possibly it was rendered more vivid by the very act of physically reproducing his narrative, a sort of uniting of your mind with his personality.

Although I've planned for a long time to get a computer, I haven't done it yet. I'm much more interested in my books. Although periodically I've given some away, the number in my bookcases stays about constant, because I keep getting more.

Al called himself a phony hermit because the very word "hermit" connotes solitude, a dislike of humanity, and probably a crotchety disposition. None of that was Al's personality. He enjoyed more visitors out on the island than he ever had here on the mainland.

You are welcome to use my letter written on the old typewriters.

I'm glad that Al's journal is being published; I think wherever he is, he knows about it and is pleased.

Sincerely,

Charlotte

Charlotte R. Seely

Al Seely died September 13, 1987 and is buried in the Pioneer or Settler's Cemetery on Bald Eagle Drive.

OBIT

Albert L. Seely

Goodland. Albert L. Seely, age 70 years passed away Tuesday at the Veterans Hospital in Miami. He came to Goodland 15 years ago from Washington D. C. and was known as "The Hermit of Dismal Key."

Survivors include a son, Mark Cowell of Melrose, MA, a sister Mrs. Erville March of Myrtle Beach, S. S.; & two grandchildren. Gravesides Services 4:00 p.m. Sunday, September 13, 1987 with the Rev. Bruce Fiol of the Marco Presbyterian church officiating, under the direction of Josberger Funeral Home.

Seely's grave at Marco Island's Pioneer Cemetery

Joe Douglas remembers Al Seely

Goodland, Florida

I do not think I should be writing these notes about Al Seely as there are many people around who knew him better. I first encountered him in Goodland in about 1980 when he was pointed out to me as being the Goodland hermit for by that time he had taken up residence in Goodland, then later in a tiny shack along with his little black dog at Margood.

Margood Trailer Park and Cottages for many years hosted mostly people coming to enjoy the warm winters of Florida living in mobile homes, and the company of many pleasant people in similar circumstances of not having a surplus of money but an abundance of fellowship.

The area supported many retirees who among them had many skills and created handcrafts and works of art. Possibly this is how I learned of Al Seely's talents as an artist. Al could be seen most days ambling along with a cane and his dog to and from the Post office. Today I am sure he would be delighted in the interior of the post office that has turned into an art gallery of fine murals and paintings by local artists. Be that as it may, by about 1986 or so, our house had been raised on pilings to be above the possibility of hurricane surges and so had a good view of the surrounding area.

Rather than install drapes that would tend to restrict the view, white shades or roll down window blinds were installed. During the day they were rolled up and were unobtrusive; but at night time the sheets of white were objectionable, so Al was asked if he would like to do something with the shades for $200 that we felt we could afford. He agreed but said he was out of paints and acetone or similar so we drove to Naples where we purchased them, plus strings for his musical instrument. Al was a pleasant, well-educated gentleman. He mentioned in passing a little about his previous life. He had been in the armed forces out in the Pacific during World War Two, I do believe in a medical capacity for which he received a small government pension of some $200 month. He was fearful of losing this if the powers that be learned of the few dollars he earned once in a while on his paintings; so he asked that I would pay him in cash. He also spoke about the fact that while in New York having been divorced twice because of his alcoholism, the doctor told him he would be dead in six months due to his drinking. That scared him so much that he realized he would have to get away from people and the temptation of booze so he resolved to escape society resulting in his life as a hermit related so interestingly by him in his tales in the Ten Thousand Islands.

As for the resulting pictures I constructed an easel for him then took the first shade to him. After some days he indicated it was finished so I took a second shade along and collected the first. I was amazed, I had not expected to receive a complete picture.

Jiver

One of the paintings was of my sailboat ~Jiver~ anchored off Panther Key where Al had lived for some five years. I gave him the photograph that he used as a guide.

Bird on Panther Key

It had been many years since he had left Panther Key but in 1980 the track he had generated on his walks to Gomez Point could still be seen skirting the mangroves also though his shack had been burned down there was still a large pile of rusted food cans.

Sunset

The painted shades were a great success and we would roll them down to show visitors, I am sure that many were envious, they, living in expensive Marco houses could not display such luxury.

Two pelicans on the dock

In all he painted six shades for me the results were so impressive that I gave him a further $100, little enough, but I suspect much more than he had received for his previous works.

Bobcat on a branch

These paintings were rolled up and down for many years but finally they were losing little patches of paint so finally they were cut out and mounted in frames to hang on my walls. Other paintings of Al's were hanging on display in the

Margood restaurant and the owners Elhanon Combs and his wife Sandy were good enough to let me photograph them.

Joe Douglas
Goodland

Joe and Ivy Douglas framed one of the picture shades to hang on the wall.

Letter from Foster Atkinson to fellow radio ham operator

Letter courtesy of Mildred Newton., Cecil Newton's daughter

E Foster Atkinson
Box 67
Goodland, Florida 33933

February 4, 1967

Station W4EBR
Cecil Newton, LBT 829
Hickory, North Carolina

Hi'ya Easy Baker Roger:

Youse guys had hardly gotten around the corner of the street that passes in front of my dock when it dawned on me what had been bugging me the most of the time we talked. I knew I was forgetting something but could not think what. After you departed I recalled I had presented a chain for a necklace, but no fastener for the chain and no "decorations" for same. The shells, etc. were intended for the ear ring. So, herewith, in three little plastic sacks I am bringing the deal up to date. Each is labeled. One contained a snap-fastener with two jump rings to attach it to the chain. Also there are 3 bell caps, each with a jump ring, plus a fourth to attach the three to the center of the chain. There are 3 catfish pearls, one for each of the bell caps. Needlenose plyers are nice to use in putting the jewelry together. Put a dot of cement (DUCO will do) in the center of the bell cap and insert the point of the pearl as deep as it will go and pinch the prongs of the cap down against the pearl and let dry. In another sack is a bracelet to match the neclace. It is ready save the cementing in of the pearls. I am out of cement at the moment, so did not do that. 'Sides, I thought you all'd get a bigger kick out of a do-it-yourself kit. The third sack contains various parts, assortments, etc. to add variety or for repairs. I cut the bracelet to fit my wrist. If large, a link or more as needed can be removed easily. Each link is split and can be twisted apart and removed. Catch on bracelet shows how to attach the one to necklace chain. Because chain of the necklace is finer, I included finer jumprings to be more in keeping.

Once again I must say I certainly enjoyed your visit out here even though short. I hope one of these days when your're in Florida again you can "camp" out here. I'm looking forward to getting together with Hanna about the 15th or 16th and then, if he can stay, add Joe Gouldsmith and Hank Mayer to the collection here. I have brought my Dismal number list up to date and Number 12 is Cecil Newton with Russ How as 11. Chances are it will say: 13—Who Cares, 14—Philip Hanna, 15—Hank Mayer if none of the wires get crossed in the meantime.

The Coffins have been out again at least 3 times during the week, including a little visit at the dock middle of the afternoon yesterday as they were on their way back from a trip to Everglades City, where they went for lunch, for a change. My neighbor Roy Osmer, finally got moved on Tuesday. Since then I have hauled two boatloads of his "left-overs" back here which includes lumber mostly, but also some hardware and electronics items.

I have quite a variety of schematics for crystal and diode short wave receivers. Some time if you can let me know your wave length and frequency I'll for fun of it try to build a little set to try to pick you up. It would be a cute trick if I could do it. I have perhaps 15 variable capacitors, but only know the *mmf* rating of one of them. I have a coil-winding slide rule to use in matching inductance and capacistance for certain frequencies and though it does not help too much when you are not sure of the value of the capacitor. I believe I also have a set of tables for various short wave frequencies so one can wind a coil to match a .00035 mmf capacitor which I can get from the outfit in California that specializes in parts and kits for Xtal sets, etc.

It is amazing how the California people boost Florida…
<u>C</u>ome
<u>A</u>nd
<u>L</u>ive
<u>I</u>n
<u>F</u>lorida   Mighty nice of them.

I'd better rush along. I am trying to get a few things done up ahead because I am seriously thinking of getting out into the mad ratrace of the world. (Goodland, only) on Monday as it is time for my pay (?) check to be in. That's even enough to drag any hermit out of seclusion and into the cruel, cruel world.

I hope you enjoyed the balance of your stay in Fla. And trust I will learn some day if you got to locate Al Hamilton in Key Largo, or if you saw Hank Mayer or Phil Hanna on your way back up state. I'll probably learn about either one of the last two when the LBT gathering takes place here a little later.

I had better close now before I get my typing arm warmed up for sure. When that happens I don't know when to stop. A big Hi to all the boys if, as, and when you see them.

73s to you and
LBTingly, eternally
E. Foster

Roy Ozmer, hermit of Pelican Key and Foster Atkinson, hermit of Panther,\ Key, - 1965.
(Photo courtesy of Everglades City High School students)

Bob Steele and the hermits of Ten Thousand Islands

May 26, 2006

I'm writing from Scott Air Force Base, where I'm stationed with the USAF. You may know my brother, Dewey Steele, of Homestead. We Steele brothers all grew up in Miami, but often spent time on Marco Island, Caxambas, the Ideal Fish Camp (it wasn't), and the Ten Thousand Islands in general from the 60s onward. I just read your article on Joe Dickman (we called him "Old Joe") and thought I'd drop you a note. I also met some of the other hermits that you write about.

Al Seely

When Al Seely lived on Panther Key, we'd visit him there and see his truly amazing collection of Calusa pottery he'd found and pieced together into complete pots! As you know, Juan/John Gomez once lived on Panther Key, and he also found artifacts from Gomez and his wife. As a young boy, this made a huge impression on me, and I always wondered what became of that pottery. When we'd visit Foster on Dismal Key, I would hike around that amazing island and often saw pottery shards on the ground in plain sight. If you look at the height of that island, it wouldn't surprise me if it had been a significant colony for the Calusa. But Dismal also had snakes, scorpions, and dark clouds of mosquitoes. I wonder if that's why it got the name Dismal.

Finally, yes, I knew about Al's struggles with alcohol. Too bad for such a smart and talented fellow.

Yes, this was Foster's house ... and later Al's house. There was a second house on the *backside* of the island .. .a shack, really. I suspect that the occasional fisherman and/or drug runners used the house. You could hike to it from Foster's place, or you could take a small boat to it. The boat was easier. If you have a copy of Charlton Tebeau's Florida's Last Frontier, he writes about a family who may have built this house. The patriarch was John Henry Thompson, a contemporary of the infamous Mr. Ed Watson. Thompson apparently built a house on Dismal Key in 1910 he moved to Caxambas and later back to Dismal. I'm guessing the house could date back that far.

I have two signed books by Charlton Tebeau. One, Man in the Everglades, had been thrown into a trash/burn pit after Foster died at his house. I happened to visit about then and retrieved it.

I've done some initial research on Dismal, traveling to the University of Florida archaeology and history depts. It seems that the only person to look at Dismal Key was Clarence B Moore. He was an amateur, however, and his papers from his digs there (circa 1901-1905) are in the Huntington Free Library in New York. That's another stop on my itinerary once I retire from the USAF next year.

As our kids were growing up, I'd tell them stories about exploring on Dismal Key. In fact, as I've considered writing "the book," I'd probably call it Dismal Key.

Dismal Key Boat House

Dismal Key House

Nelson Barlow and I built that for Foster to keep his boat out of the weather and away from thieves in around 1969/1970. When we were at Dismal for Nelson's memorial service last Sept 05, I noticed that it's in pieces, likely from a storm, vandals, or both. The house was burned down, I think by the 10,000 islands park folks. The only structure still there is the cistern.

Nelson "Nels" Barlow

Nelson Barlow was like a father figure to the Steele family and you are right ... he was an amazing person. He rode a bicycle from Richmond to Miami in the 30s and the inventor (patent holding) of several innovations at the Miami Herald over 30 or so years. He built the houseboat in his suburban Miami back yard--it weighed over 9 tons--then disassembled it after carefully marking every piece. Reassembled it at Lawrence Pettit's Ideal Fish Camp and later relocated it to Dismal Key in the late 60s. We had many a family gathering on "SEASAH," a name coined by Foster Atkinson that stood for the "Society for Elimination of All Smart-A**ed Hermits."

I used to go pin-fishing with Babo and Jane (Ludlow) when I was a kid. Our friend Nelson Barlow would host many of the locals on his houseboat, first built and anchored at the Ideal Fish Camp, then in the Caxambas area, and then at Dismal Key. I used to stay on the houseboat when Nelson had it anchored at Helen Key, Horr's Island, and Dismal Key.

Nelson's Houseboat Seasah at Dismal Key

Al Seely, Foster Atkinson, Joe Dickman

Nelson Barlow & Bob Steele aboard a rented houseboat near Cape Romano in 1997. It was a Steele family reunion & Nelson is retelling me a story or two

I also spent quite a bit of time at Dismal Key when Foster Atkinson lived there from 1957 to about 1971, followed by Al Seely, then Jerry, then Naranjan. Have you ever written or researched on the people who have lived on Dismal Key? I believe that a family named Thompson built the house that the hermits lived in maybe in the '20s or '30s. It's gone now. We recently visited Dismal when our dear family friend, Nelson Barlow, passed away. Mr. Barlow was most responsible for teaching us about the Ten Thousand Islands. He was our guide, navigator, and mentor on the area. He built the houseboat SEASAH that was anchored at Dismal Key and elsewhere before it sunk in Hurricane Andrew. When he passed away, we spread his ashes in Dismal Channel at his request and I got to see the island for the first time in nearly 20 years. It looks like as if it is reverting to its natural state, which I guess isn't a bad thing.

On Joe Dickman, hermit of Kice Island

I met Joe in 1965 when I was about 8 years old. He was still living in the old Barfield house with another man named Charlie. Charlie was the bartender for Lawrence Pettit at the Ideal Fish Camp. I remember he was bald with a goatee. Nice guy. Both had moved to the lower parts of the house as the roof had big open holes in it and they were escaping the rain and mosquitoes. Later, he lived in a trailer on the site of the house it seems to me. I remember when the house burned down. Joe told me a story about leaving his house in Kice Island DURING hurricane Donna in 1960; quite the tale.

Old Joe told me he greatly underestimated Hurricane Donna in 1960. He chose to ride the storm out on Kice Island but only made it through the first half of the storm before his house started coming apart. During the eye's passing, the surge, as he described it, took the water OUT of Caxambas Pass. He then, in a panic, WALKED from the remains of his house on Kice Island to Marco, seeking shelter in the Barfield house on high ground. I always imagined more of a "wading" across, but he said he walked it. Hard to imagine, I know. He lived there or in a trailer nearby until his death. I'd be

interested in hearing if any of the old timers recall Caxambas Pass being "dry" during Donna (not that anyone would be out looking!).

I was always fascinated by the stone remains of Joe's house on Kice Island and the artesian well that spilled fresh water into Caxambas Pass. Those have both been washed away as Kice erodes southward.

Foster Atkinson, on Dismal Key, reported the water ROSE there about 12 feet, coming up the hill to his house, but never really threatening him (the shell mound where the house used to be is about 20 feet above sea level).

Dickman on Nels houseboat – 1960

Following In Al Seely's Boot Prints
Betsy Perdichizzi

Shortly before the publication of Al Seely's memoirs, Nancy Nalley and Martin Reeb were our guides to the backwaters of the Ten Thousand Islands to see the keys where Al Seely spent ten years of his life.

Nancy Nalley, a biologist, along with Elizabeth and Mike Langston, worked on a hurricane grant for the federal government in 1995. Nancy monitored the bays, inlets and keys for several years. Martin surveyed the elevations for the hurricane grant.

On a clear, sunny Saturday morning, my husband Bill and I set out with our friends in their 17-foot Montauk, a Boston Whaler, loaded down with sandwiches, fresh fruit, chips, smoked oysters and bottles of water that Nancy had provided for the trip. We supplied the bug spray and sun block.

Nancy said that because it was low tide, she planned to take the outer route by Coon Key Light, and to return the inside route across the shallow Shell Key Bay. She said it was about 1 ½ hours from her home which seemed incredible to us who are used to going by sail where it takes all day to get anywhere.

We passed under the Barfield bridge and made our way out and around the ABC bird islands where we picked up the Marco River heading toward Goodland. We traveled under the big high-rise Goodland Bridge into Goodland Bay. The bridge replaced the old, low Goodland Swing Bridge in 1975, while Seely was living on Panther Key.

As we rounded scenic Goodland Point, I asked Nancy to show us the channel where Al Seely might have put in to pick up supplies, mail, and occasional booze. Slowing down, she indicated the waterway leading to a small bay behind MarGood store. The Goodland Post Office is just a across the way. Nancy indicated that he might have used a smaller inlet to the west that led to another little store in the 70's

We saw many birds: Ospreys seemed to have nested on every marker, and Great Blue Herons and White Herons were fishing in and around the stark mangrove roots looking like pretty small statues. Boat traffic was light, but there were campers and sightseers on some of the keys and beaches. According to Nancy, many of the beaches were new since Hurricane Wilma and would not have been there in Seely's day.

From the Coon Key Light in Gullivan's Bay we could see tiny Brush Key where Seely tent camped for seven months, in the first part of his hermitdom.

Next we stopped at Panther Key to take pictures; and they said we might go ashore if we didn't mind getting our feet wet.

Nancy and Martin anchored near the site of the old boathouse and we climbed the steep pathway leading up the 16-foot shell mound hill toward the old house. The house is not there anymore. Nancy explained that the Federal Government acquired these keys from the Collier Company in a great land swap. To protect and preserve the fragile areas, the government burned all the shacks down, including the sixty-year-old split-level house where more than one hermit lived.

As we climbed ashore, she warned us to watch out for rattlesnakes on the island. "There are large ones here and I have seen them." Having forgotten her snake stick, she armed herself with a paddle from the boat." She explained that Rattlesnakes are now on the endangered species list in Florida and you can't kill them as Seely did.

We followed the path up the hill through a cactus patch, winding in and around shrubbery, beneath Satin Leaf trees, and undergrowth.

Nancy Nalley, expedition leader with snake stick paddle

Bill took a picture of the old cistern

We saw a collapsed roofed building that may have been an outhouse.

An iron relic was rusting away amid the piles of old bottles and trash; no one knew how it got there, or what it was used for.

We smelled the White Stopper tree with its skunk-like odor, but we didn't see one.

As we made our way down, I tried to imagine Al and Foster before him, passing days, months and years in this solitary, green place amidst nature in all its elements. It must have been remarkable experience, I am glad that he wrote about it.

We boarded the boat and motored around to Dismal Key to find Gomez Point jutting out into the water, looking as it has looked for many years. With its long beach, the island is still a popular place to visit and camp.